AJESH FAIZAL
VUGAR ABDULLAYEV

STORAGE AREA NETWORKS

AJESH FAIZAL
VUGAR ABDULLAYEV

STORAGE AREA NETWORKS

DESIGN, PRINCIPLES & MANAGEMENT

Noor Publishing

Imprint

Any brand names and product names mentioned in this book are subject to trademark, brand or patent protection and are trademarks or registered trademarks of their respective holders. The use of brand names, product names, common names, trade names, product descriptions etc. even without a particular marking in this work is in no way to be construed to mean that such names may be regarded as unrestricted in respect of trademark and brand protection legislation and could thus be used by anyone.

Cover image: www.ingimage.com

Publisher:
Noor Publishing
is a trademark of
Dodo Books Indian Ocean Ltd. and OmniScriptum S.R.L publishing group

120 High Road, East Finchley, London, N2 9ED, United Kingdom
Str. Armeneasca 28/1, office 1, Chisinau MD-2012, Republic of Moldova, Europe
Printed at: see last page
ISBN: 978-620-5-63904-7

STORAGE AREA NETWORKS
DESIGN, PRINCIPLES & MANAGEMENT

AJESH FAIZAL

Associate Professor, Department of Computer Science and Engineering, Sree Buddha College of Engineering, Pattoor, Alappuzha, Kerala, India

VUGAR ABDULLAYEV

Associate Professor, Department of Computer Engineering, Azerbaijan State Oil & Industry University ,Baku, Azerbaijan

ACKNOWLEDGEMENT

From the depths of our hearts, we offer our deepest gratitude to The Almighty for the countless blessings bestowed upon us throughout the journey of crafting this book. His divine guidance and unwavering support provided the strength and clarity needed to bring this project to fruition.

We extend our sincerest appreciation to the esteemed Chairman of the Sree Buddha Group of Institutions, **Prof. K. Sasikumar.** His unwavering faith in our vision and his full support throughout the writing process were instrumental in the book's completion. We are deeply grateful for his leadership and dedication to advancing education.

We are also incredibly thankful to the esteemed Principal, **Dr. K. Krishna Kumar**, for his constant guidance and encouragement. His insightful feedback and unwavering support proved invaluable in shaping the content and ensuring its clarity. We are truly fortunate to have benefited from his expertise.

A heartfelt thank you goes out to our esteemed colleagues for their unwavering support and encouragement throughout this endeavor. Their belief in our work and their willingness to share their knowledge fueled our motivation and ensured a collaborative environment.

This journey also provides an opportunity to express our gratitude to all those who, directly or indirectly, played a role in the successful completion of this book. Their contributions, both large and small, are deeply appreciated.

Finally, we recognize the dedication of **the Azerbaijan State Oil & Industry University** in Baku, Azerbaijan, to advancing technical education on a global scale. Their commitment to fostering knowledge and expertise undoubtedly played a part in the creation and dissemination of valuable resources such as this one.

TABLE OF CONTENTS

UNIT-I

STORAGE SYSTEM

1.1 Introduction to Information storage

1.1.1 Why Information management?

- Information is increasingly important in our daily lives. We have become information Dependents.
- We live in on-command, on-demand world that means we need information when and where it is required.
- We access the Internet every day to perform searches, participate in social networking, send and receive e-mails, share pictures and videos, and scores of other applications. Equipped with a growing number of content-generating devices, more information is being created by individuals than by businesses.
- The importance, dependency, and volume of information for the business world also continue to grow at astounding rates.
- Businesses depend on fast and reliable access to information critical to their success. Some of the business applications that process information include airline reservations, telephone billing systems, e-commerce, ATMs, product designs, inventory management, e-mail archives, Web portals, patient records, credit cards, life sciences, and global capital markets.
- The increasing criticality of information to the businesses has amplified the challenges in protecting and managing the data.
- Organizations maintain one or more data centers to store and manage information. A data center is a facility that contains information storage and other physical information technology (IT) resources for computing, networking, and storing information.

1.1.2 Information Storage

Businesses use data to derive information that is critical to their day-to-day operations. Storage is a repository that enables users to store and retrieve this digital data.

Data

- Data is a collection of raw facts from which conclusions may be drawn.

➢ Eg: a printed book, a family photograph, a movie on videotape, e-mail message, an e-book, a bitmapped image, or a digital movie are all examples of data.

➢ The data can be generated using a computer and stored in strings of 0s and 1s(as shown in Fig 1.1), is called digital data and is accessible by the user only after it is processed by a computer.

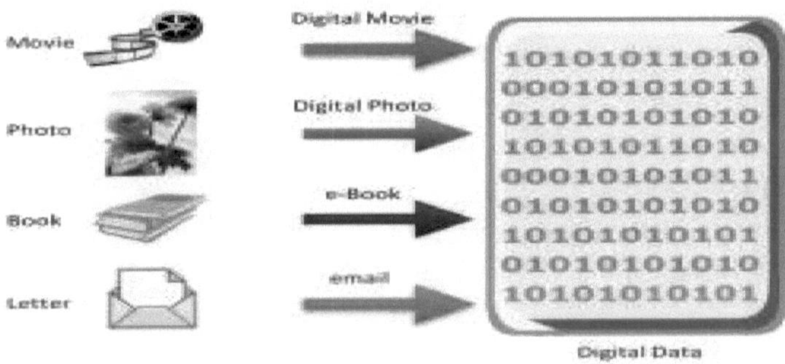

Fig 1.1: Digital data

The following is a list of some of the factors that have contributed to the growth of digital data :

1. **Increase in data processing capabilities**: Modern-day computers provide a significant increase in processing and storage capabilities. This enables the conversion of various types of content and media from conventional forms to digital formats.

2. **Lower cost of digital storage:** Technological advances and decrease in the cost of storage devices have provided low-cost solutions and encouraged the development of less expensive data storage devices. This cost benefit has increased the rate at which data is being generated and stored.

3. **Affordable and faster communication technology:** The rate of sharing digital data is now much faster than traditional approaches. A handwritten letter may take a week to reach its destination, whereas it only takes a few seconds for an e-mail message to reach its recipient.

4. **Proliferation of applications and smart devices:** Smartphones, tablets, and newer digitaldevices, along with smart applications, have significantly contributed to the generation of digital content.

1.1.3 Types of Data

Data can be classified as structured or unstructured (see Fig 1.2) based on how it is stored and managed.

- ➤ **Structured data:**
  - Structured data is organized in rows and columns in a rigidly defined format so that applications can retrieve and process it efficiently.
  - Structured data is typically stored using a database management system (DBMS).
- ➤ **Unstructured data:**
  - Data is unstructured if its elements cannot be stored in rows and columns, and is therefore difficult to query and retrieve by business applications.
  - Example: e-mail messages, business cards, or even digital format files such as .doc, .txt, and .pdf.

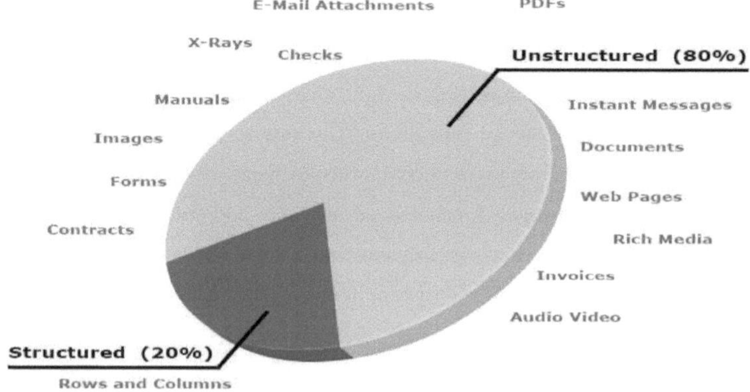

Fig 1.2: Types of data

1.1.4 Big Data

- ➤ Big data refers to data sets whose sizes are beyond the capability of commonly used software tools to capture, store, manage, and process within acceptable time limits.

> It includes both structured and unstructured data generated by a variety of sources, including business application transactions, web pages, videos, images, e-mails, social media, and so on.

> The big data ecosystem (see Fig 1.3) consists of the following:

  1. Devices that collect data from multiple locations and also generate new data about this data (metadata).

  2. Data collectors who gather data from devices and users.

  3. Data aggregators that compile the collected data to extract meaningful information.

  4. Data users and buyers who benefit from the information collected and aggregated by others in the data value chain .

Fig 1.3: Big data Ecosystem

> Big data Analysis in real time requires new techniques, architectures, and tools that provide :

  1. high performance,

  2. massively parallel processing (MPP) data platforms,

  3. advanced analytics on the data sets.

> Big data Analytics provide an opportunity to translate large volumes of data into right decisions.

1.1.5 Information

> Data, whether structured or unstructured, does not fulfil any purpose for individuals or businesses unless it is presented in a meaningful form.

- Information is the intelligence and knowledge derived from data.
- Businesses analyze raw data in order to identify meaningful trends. On the basis of these trends, a company can plan or modify its strategy.
- For example, a retailer identifies customers' preferred products and brand names by analyzing their purchase patterns and maintaining an inventory of those products.
- Because information is critical to the success of a business, there is an ever present concern about its availability and protection.

1.1.6 Storage

- Data created by individuals or businesses must be stored so that it is easily accessible for further processing.
- In a computing environment, devices designed for storing data are termed storage devices or simply storage.
- The type of storage used varies based on the type of data and the rate at which it is created and used.
  - Devices such as memory in a cell phone or digital camera, DVDs, CD-ROMs, and hard disks in personal computers are examples of storage devices.
- Businesses have several options available for storing data including internal hard disks, external disk arrays and tapes.

1.2 Introduction to Evolution of Storage Architecture

- Historically, organizations had centralized computers (mainframe) and information storage devices (tape reels and disk packs) in their data center.
- The evolution of open systems and the affordability and ease of deployment that they offer made it possible for business units/departments to have their own servers and storage.
- In earlier implementations of open systems, the storage was typically internal to the server. This approach is referred to as **server-centric storage architecture** (see Fig 1.4 [a]).
- In this server-centric storage architecture, each server has a limited number of storage devices, and any administrative tasks, such as maintenance of the server or increasing storage capacity, might result in unavailability of information.
- The rapid increase in the number of departmental servers in an enterprise resulted in

unprotected, unmanaged, fragmented islands of information and increased capital and operating expenses.

> To overcome these challenges, storage evolved from **server-centric to information-centric architecture** (see Fig 1.4 [b]).

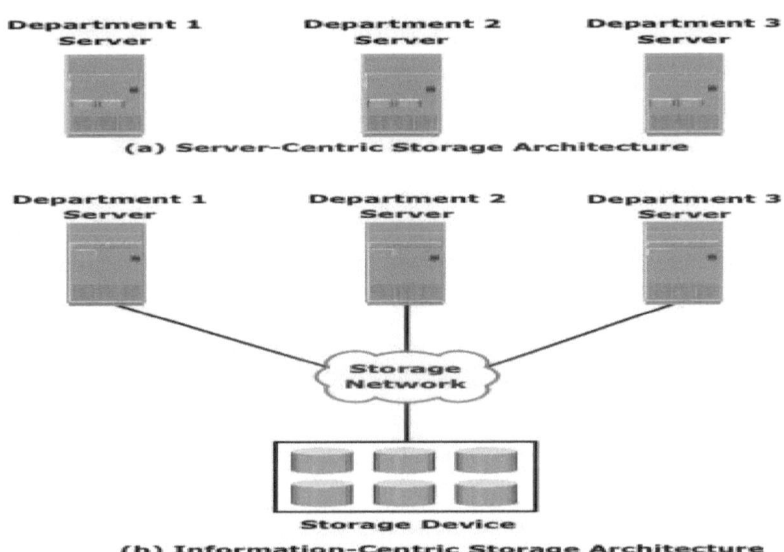

Fig 1.4: Evolution of storage architecture

> In information-centric architecture, storage devices are managed centrally and independent of servers.

> These centrally-managed storage devices are shared with multiple servers.

> When a new server is deployed in the environment, storage is assigned from the same shared storage devices to that server.

> The capacity of shared storage can be increased dynamically by adding more storage devices without impacting information availability.

> In this architecture, information management is easier and cost-effective.

> Storage technology and architecture continues to evolve, which enables organizations to

consolidate, protect, optimize, and leverage their data to achieve the highest return on information assets.

1.3 Data Center Infrastructure

- ➢ Organizations maintain data centers to provide centralized data processing capabilities across the enterprise.
- ➢ The data center infrastructure includes computers, storage systems, network devices, dedicated power backups, and environmental controls (such as air conditioning and fire suppression).

1.3.1 Key Data Center Elements

Five core elements are essential for the basic functionality of a data center:

1) **Application:** An application is a computer program that provides the logic for computing operations. Eg: order processing system.
2) **Database:** More commonly, a database management system (DBMS) provides a structured way to store data in logically organized tables that are interrelated. A DBMS optimizes the storage and retrieval of data.
3) **Host or compute:** A computing platform (hardware, firmware, and software) that runs applications and databases.
4) **Network:** A data path that facilitates communication among various networked devices.
5) **Storage array:** A device that stores data persistently for subsequent use.

- ➢ These core elements are typically viewed and managed as separate entities, but all the elements must work together to address data processing requirements.
- ➢ Fig 1.5 shows an example of an order processing system that involves the five core elements of a data center and illustrates their functionality in a business process.
  1) A customer places an order through a client machine connected over a LAN/ WAN to a host running an order-processing application.
  2) The client accesses the DBMS on the host through the application to provide order-related information, such as the customer name, address, payment method, products ordered, and quantity ordered.

3) The DBMS uses the host operating system to write this data to the database located on physical disks in the storage array.

4) The Storage Network provides the communication link between the host and the storage array and transports the request to read or write commands between them.

5) The storage array, after receiving the read or write request from the host, performs the necessary operations to store the data on physical disks.

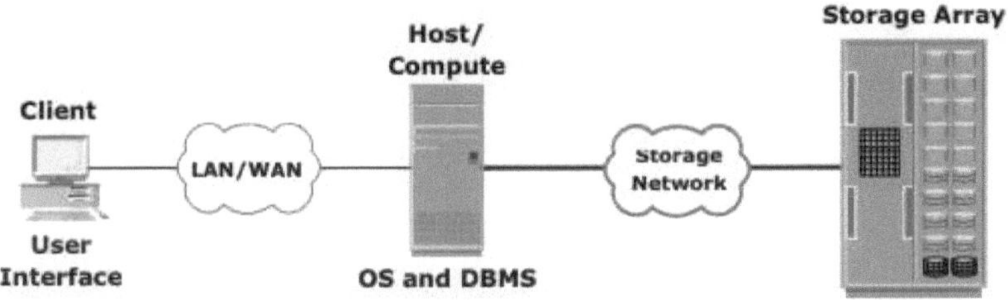

Fig 1.5: Example of an online order transaction system

1.4 Key characteristics for Data Center Elements

Key characteristics of data center elements are:

1) **Availability:** All data center elements should be designed to ensure accessibility. The inability of users to access data can have a significant negative impact on a business.

2) **Security:** Polices, procedures, and proper integration of the data center core elements that will prevent unauthorized access to information must be established. Specific mechanisms must enable servers to access only their allocated resources on storage arrays.

3) **Scalability:** Data center operations should be able to allocate additional processing capabilities (eg: servers, new applications, and additional databases) or storage on demand, without interrupting business operations. The storage solution should be able to grow with the business.

4) **Performance**: All the core elements of the data center should be able to provide optimal performance and service all processing requests at high speed. The infrastructure should be able to support performance requirements.

5) **Data integrity:** Data integrity refers to mechanisms such as error correction codes or parity bits which ensure that data is written to disk exactly as it was received. Any variation in data during its retrieval implies corruption, which may affect the operations of the organization.

6) **Capacity:** Data center operations require adequate resources to store and process large amounts of data efficiently. When capacity requirements increase, the data center must be able to provide additional capacity without interrupting availability, or, at the very least, with minimal disruption. Capacity may be managed by reallocation of existing resources, rather than by adding new resources.

7) **Manageability:** A data center should perform all operations and activities in the most efficient manner. Manageability can be achieved through automation and the reduction of human (manual) intervention in common tasks.

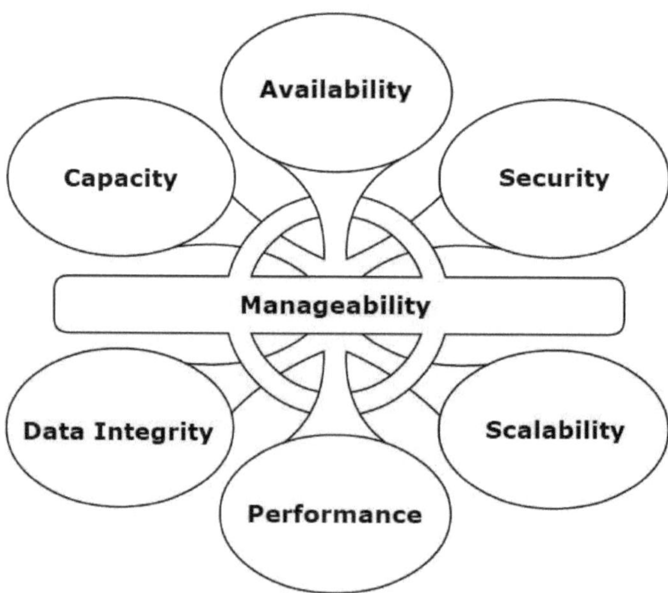

Fig 1.6: Key characteristics of data center elements

1.5 Virtualization

- Virtualization is a technique of abstracting physical resources, such as compute, storage, and network, and making them appear as logical resources.
- Virtualization has existed in the IT industry for several years and in different forms.
- Common examples of virtualization are virtual memory used on compute systems and partitioning of raw disks.
- Virtualization enables pooling of physical resources and providing an aggregated view of the physical resource capabilities. For example, storage virtualization enables multiple pooled storage devices to appear as a single large storage entity.
- Similarly, by using compute virtualization, the CPU capacity of the pooled physical servers can be viewed as the aggregation of the power of all CPUs (in megahertz).
- Virtualization also enables centralized management of pooled resources.
- Virtual resources can be created and provisioned from the pooled physical resources. For example, a virtual disk of a given capacity can be created from a storage pool or a virtual server with specific CPU power and memory can be configured from a compute pool.
- These virtual resources share pooled physical resources, which improves the utilization of physical IT resources.
- Based on business requirements, capacity can be added to or removed from the virtual resources without any disruption to applications or users.
- With improved utilization of IT assets, organizations save the costs associated management of new physical resources. Moreover, fewer physical resources means less space and energy, which leads to better economics and green computing.

1.6 Cloud Computing

- Cloud computing enables individuals or businesses to use IT resources as a service over the network.
- It provides highly scalable and flexible computing that enables provisioning of resources on demand.
- Users can scale up or scale down the demand of computing resources, including storage

capacity, with minimal management effort or service provider interaction.

➢ Cloud computing empowers self-service requesting through a fully automated request-fulfillment process.

➢ Cloud computing enables consumption-based metering; therefore, consumers pay only for the resources they use, such as CPU hours used, amount of data transferred, and gigabytes of data stored.

➢ Cloud infrastructure is usually built upon virtualized data centers, which provide resource pooling and rapid provisioning of resources.

1.7 Key Data center Elements

1.7.1 Application
➢ An application is a computer program that provides the logic for computing operations.

➢ The application sends requests to the underlying operating system to perform read/write (R/W) operations on the storage devices.

➢ Applications deployed in a data center environment are commonly categorized as business applications, infrastructure management applications, data protection applications, and security applications.

➢ Some examples of these applications are e-mail, enterprise resource planning (ERP), decision support system (DSS), resource management, backup, authentication and antivirus applications, and so on

1.7.2. DBMS

➢ A database is a structured way to store data in logically organized tables that are interrelated.

➢ A DBMS controls the creation, maintenance, and use of a database.

1.7.3 Host(or) Compute

➢ The computers on which applications run are referred to as hosts. Hosts can range from simple laptops to complex clusters of servers.

➢ Hosts can be physical or virtual machines.

➢ A compute virtualization software enables creating virtual machines on top of a physical compute infrastructure.

> A host consists of

✓ CPU: The CPU consists of four components-Arithmetic Logic Unit (ALU), control unit, registers, and L1 cache

✓ Memory: There are two types of memory on a host, Random Access Memory (RAM) and Read-Only Memory (ROM)

✓ I/O devices : keyboard, mouse, monitor

✓ a collection of software to perform computing operations- This software includes the operating system, file system, logical volume manager, device drivers, and so on.

The following section details various software components that are essential parts of a host system.

1.7.3.1 Operating System

> In a traditional computing environment, an operating system controls all aspects of computing.

> It works between the application and the physical components of a compute system.

> In a virtualized compute environment, the virtualization layer works between the operating system and the hardware resources.

Functions of OS

> data access
> monitors and responds to user actions and the environment
> organizes and controls hardware components
> manages the allocation of hardware resources
> It provides basic security for the access and usage of all managed resources
> performs basic storage management tasks
> manages the file system, volume manager, and device drivers.

Memory Virtualization

> Memory has been, and continues to be, an expensive component of a host.
> It determines both the size and number of applications that can run on a host.
> Memory virtualization is an operating system feature that virtualizes the physical memory

(RAM) of a host.

- ➢ It creates virtual memory with an address space larger than the physical memory space present in the compute system.
- ➢ The operating system utility that manages the virtual memory is known as the virtual memory manager (VMM).
- ➢ The space used by the VMM on the disk is known as a swap space.
- ➢ A swap space (also known as page file or swap file) is a portion of the disk drive that appears to be physical memory to the operating system.
- ➢ In a virtual memory implementation, the memory of a system is divided into contiguous blocks of fixed-size pages.
- ➢ A process known as paging moves inactive physical memory pages onto the swap file and brings them back to the physical memory when required.

1.7.3.2 Device Drivers

- ➢ A device driver is special software that permits the operating system to interact with a specific device, such as a printer, a mouse, or a disk drive.

1.7.3.3 Volume Manager

- ➢ In the early days, disk drives appeared to the operating system as a number of continuous disk blocks. The entire disk drive would be allocated to the file system or other data entity used by the operating system or application.

Disadvantages:

- ✓ lack of flexibility.
- ✓ When a disk drive ran out of space, there was no easy way to extend the file system's size.
- ✓ as the storage capacity of the disk drive increased, allocating the entire disk drive for the file system often resulted in underutilization of storage capacity

Solution: evolution of Logical Volume Managers (LVMs)

- ➢ LVM enabled dynamic extension of file system capacity and efficient storage management.

Storage Area Networks

- The LVM is software that runs on the compute system and manages logical and physical storage.
- LVM is an intermediate layer between the file system and the physical disk.
- LVM can partition a larger-capacity disk into virtual, smaller-capacity volumes(called Partitioning) or aggregate several smaller disks to form a larger virtual volume. The process is called concatenation.
- Disk partitioning was introduced to improve the flexibility and utilization of disk drives.
- In partitioning, a disk drive is divided into logical containers called logical volumes (LVs) (see Fig 1.7)

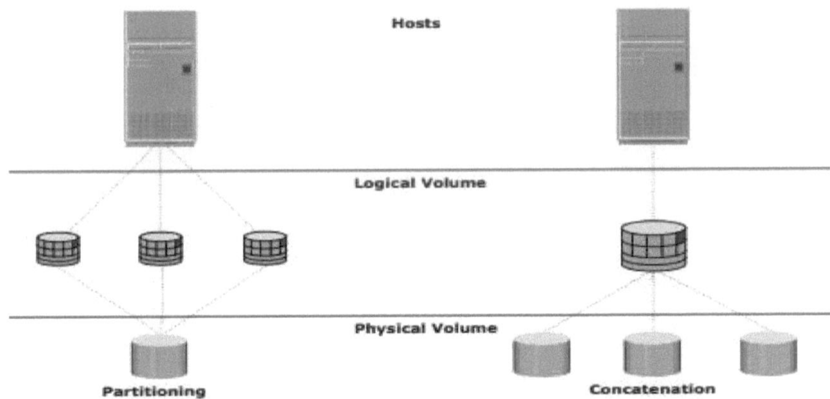

Fig 1.7: Disk Partitioning and concatenation

- Concatenation is the process of grouping several physical drives and presenting them to the host as one big logical volume.
- The basic LVM components are **physical volumes, volume groups, and logical volumes**.
- Each physical disk connected to the host system is a **physical volume (PV).**
- A **volume group** is created by grouping together one or more physical volumes. A unique physical volume identifier (PVID) is assigned to each physical volume when it is initialized for use by the LVM. Each physical volume is partitioned into equal-sized data blocks called **physical extents** when the volume group is created.

- ➢ **Logical volumes** are created within a given volume group. A logical volume can be thought of as a disk partition, whereas the volume group itself can be thought of as a disk.

1.7.3.4 File System

- ➢ A file is a **collection of related records** or data stored as a unit with a name.
- ➢ A file system is a hierarchical structure of files.
- ➢ A file system enables easy access to data files residing within a disk drive, a disk partition, or a logical volume.
- ➢ It provides users with the functionality to create, modify, delete, and access files.
- ➢ Access to files on the disks is controlled by the permissions assigned to the file by the owner, which are also maintained by the file system.
- ➢ A file system organizes data in a structured hierarchical manner via the use of directories, which are containers for storing pointers to multiple files.
- ➢ All file systems maintain a pointer map to the directories, subdirectories, and files that are part of the file system.
- ➢ Examples of common file systems are:

    - ✓ FAT 32 (File Allocation Table) for Microsoft Windows
    - ✓ NT File System (NTFS) for Microsoft Windows
    - ✓ UNIX File System (UFS) for UNIX
    - ✓ Extended File System (EXT2/3) for Linux

- ➢ The file system also includes a number of other related records, which are collectively called the **metadata**.
- ➢ For example, the metadata in a UNIX environment consists of the **superblock, the inodes, and the list of data blocks free and in use.**
- ➢ A superblock contains important information about the file system, such as the file system type, creation and modification dates, size, and layout.
- ➢ An inode is associated with every file and directory and contains information such as the file length, ownership, access privileges, time of last access/modification, number of links, and the address of the data.
- ➢ A file system block is the smallest "unit" allocated for storing data.

➢ The following list shows the process of mapping user files to the disk storage subsystem with an LVM (see Fig 1.8)

    1. Files are created and managed by users and applications.

    2. These files reside in the file systems.

    3. The file systems are mapped to file system blocks.

    4. The file system blocks are mapped to logical extents of a logical volume.

    5. These logical extents in turn are mapped to the disk physical extents either by the operating system or by the LVM.

    6. These physical extents are mapped to the disk sectors in a storage subsystem.

If there is no LVM, then there are no logical extents. Without LVM, file system blocks are directly mapped to disk sectors.

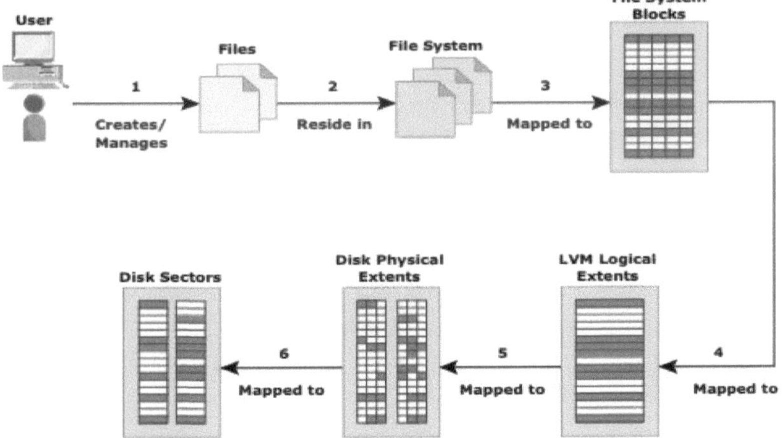

Fig 1.8: Process of mapping user files to disk storage

➢ The file system tree starts with the root directory. The root directory has a number of subdirectories.

➢ A file system can be either :

    ✓ a journaling file system

    ✓ a nonjournaling file system.

Nonjournaling file system : Nonjournaling file systems cause a potential loss of files because they use separate writes to update their data and metadata. If the system crashes during the write process, the metadata or data might be lost or corrupted. When the system reboots, the file system attempts to update the metadata structures by examining and repairing them. This operation takes a long time on large file systems. If there is insufficient information to re-create the wanted or original structure, the files might be misplaced or lost, resulting in corrupted file systems.

Journaling file system: Journaling File System uses a separate area called a *log* or *journal*. This journal might contain all the data to be written (physical journal) or just the metadata to be updated (logical journal). Before changes are made to the file system, they are written to this separate area. After the journal has been updated, the operation on the file system can be performed. If the system crashes during the operation, there is enough information in the log to "*replay*" the log record and complete the operation. Nearly all file system implementations today use journaling

Advantages:

➢ Journaling results in a quick file system check because it looks only at the active, most recently accessed parts of a large file system.

➢ Since information about the pending operation is saved, the risk of files being lost is reduced.

Disadvantage:

➢ they are slower than other file systems. This slowdown is the result of the extra operations that have to be performed on the journal each time the file system is changed.

➢ But the advantages of lesser time for file system checks and maintaining file system integrity far outweighs its disadvantage.

1.7.3.5 Compute Virtualization

➢ Compute virtualization is a technique for *masking* or *abstracting* the physical hardware from the operating system. It enables multiple operating systems to run concurrently on single or clustered physical machines.

➢ This technique enables creating portable virtual compute systems called *virtual machines* (VMs) running its own operating system and application instance in an isolated manner.

➢ Compute virtualization is achieved by a virtualization layer that resides between the hardware and virtual machines called the *hypervisor*. The hypervisor provides hardware resources, such as CPU, memory, and network to all the virtual machines.

➢ A virtual machine is a logical entity but appears like a physical host to the operating system, with its own CPU, memory, network controller, and disks. However, all VMs share the same underlying physical hardware in an isolated manner.

➢ Before Compute virtualization:

    ✓ A physical server often faces resource-conflict issues when two or more applications running on the same server have conflicting requirements. As a result, only one application can be run on a server at a time, as shown in Fig 1.9 (a).

    ✓ Due to this, organizations will need to purchase new physical machines for every application they deploy, resulting in expensive and inflexible infrastructure.

    ✓ Many applications do not fully utilize complete hardware capabilities available to them. Resources such as processors, memory and storage remain underutilized.

    ✓ Compute virtualization enables users to overcome these challenges (see Fig 1.9 (b)).

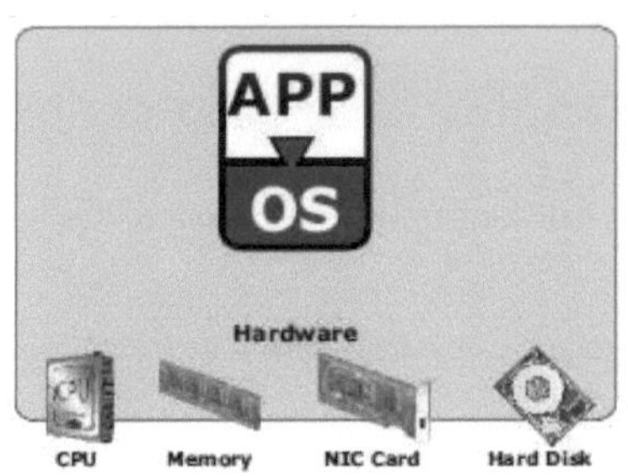

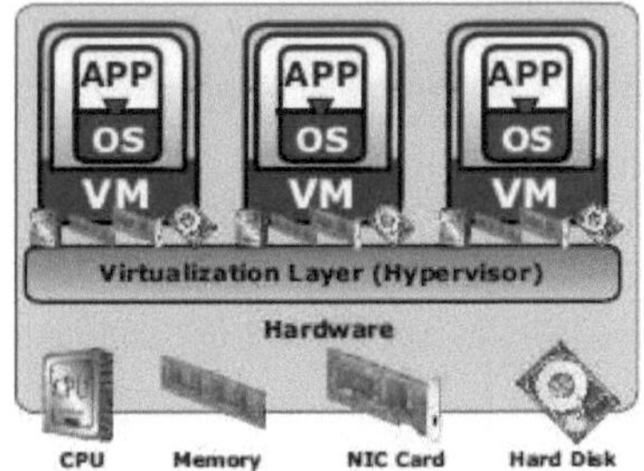

Fig 1.9: Server Virtualization

➢ After Compute virtualization:

    ✓ This technique significantly improves server utilization and provides server consolidation.

    ✓ *Server consolidation* enables organizations to run their data center with fewer physical servers.

    ✓ This, in turn,

- reduces cost of new server acquisition,
        - reduces operational cost,
        - saves data center floor and rack space.
    ✓ Individual VMs can be restarted, upgraded, or even crashed, without affecting the other VMs.
    ✓ VMs can be copied or moved from one physical machine to another (non-disruptive migration) without causing application downtime. This is required for maintenance activities

1.8 Connectivity

➤ Connectivity refers to the interconnection between hosts or between a host and peripheral devices, such as printers or storage devices.
➤ Connectivity and communication between host and storage are enabled using:
    ✓ physical components
    ✓ interface protocols.

1.8.1 Physical Components of Connectivity

➤ The physical components of connectivity are the hardware elements that connect the host to storage.
➤ Three physical components of connectivity between the host and storage are (refer Fig 1.10):
    ✓ the host interface device
    ✓ port
    ✓ cable.

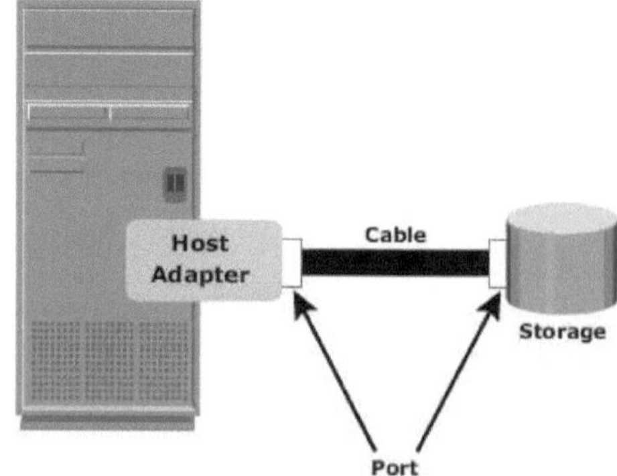

Fig 1.10: Physical components of connectivity

- A *host interface device* or *host adapter* connects a host to other hosts and storage devices.
    - ✓ Eg: host bus adapter (HBA) and network interface card (NIC).
    - ✓ HBA is an application-specific integrated circuit (ASIC) board that performs I/O interface functions between the host and storage, relieving the CPU from additional I/O processing workload.
    - ✓ A host typically contains multiple HBAs.
- A *port* is a specialized outlet that enables connectivity between the host and external devices. An HBA may contain one or more ports to connect the host.
- *Cables* connect hosts to internal or external devices using copper or fiber optic media.

1.8.2 Interface Protocols

- A protocol enables communication between the host and storage.
- Protocols are implemented using interface devices (or controllers) at both source and destination.
- The popular interface protocols used for host to storage communications are:
    i. Integrated Device Electronics/Advanced Technology Attachment (IDE/ATA)
    ii. Small Computer System Interface (SCSI),
    iii. Fibre Channel (FC)
    iv. Internet Protocol (IP)

IDE/ATA and Serial ATA:
- **IDE/ATA** is a popular interface protocol standard used for connecting storage devices, such as disk drives and CD-ROM drives.
- This protocol supports parallel transmission and therefore is also known as *Parallel ATA (PATA)* or simply ATA.
- IDE/ATA has a variety of standards and names.
- The Ultra DMA/133 version of ATA supports a throughput of **133 MB per second**.
- In a master-slave configuration, an ATA interface supports two storage devices per connector.
- If performance of the drive is important, sharing a port between two devices is not

recommended.

- ➤ The serial version of this protocol is known as Serial ATA (SATA) and supports single bit serial transmission.
- ➤ *High performance* and *low cost* SATA has replaced PATA in newer systems.
- ➤ SATA revision 3.0 provides a data transfer rate up to **6 Gb/s.**

SCSI and Serial SCSI:

- ➤ **SCSI** has emerged as a preferred connectivity protocol in high-end computers.
- ➤ This protocol supports parallel transmission and offers improved **performance, scalability, and compatibility** compared to ATA.
- ➤ The high cost associated with SCSI limits its popularity among home or personal desktop users.
- ➤ SCSI supports up to 16 devices on a single bus and provides data transfer rates up to **640 MB/s.**
- ➤ **Serial attached SCSI (SAS)** is a point-to-point serial protocol that provides an alternative to parallel SCSI.
- ➤ A newer version of serial SCSI (SAS 2.0) supports a data transfer rate up to **6 Gb/s.**

Fibre Channel (FC):

- ➤ **Fibre Channel** is a widely used protocol for high-speed communication to the storage device.
- ➤ Fibre Channel interface provides gigabit network speed.
- ➤ It provides a serial data transmission that operates over copper wire and optical fiber.
- ➤ The latest version of the FC interface (16FC) allows transmission of data up to **16 Gb/s.**

Internet Protocol (IP):

- ➤ IP is a network protocol that has been traditionally used for **host-to-host traffic**.
- ➤ With the emergence of new technologies, an IP network has become a viable option for host-to-storage communication.
- ➤ IP offers several advantages:
    - ✓ cost
    - ✓ maturity

✓ enables organizations to leverage their existing IP-based network.

- ➢ **iSCSI** and **FCIP** protocols are common examples that leverage IP for host-to-storage communication.

1.9 Storage

- ➢ Storage is a core component in a data center.
- ➢ A storage device uses magnetic, optic, or solid state media.
- ➢ Disks, tapes, and diskettes use magnetic media,
- ➢ CD/DVD uses optical media.
- ➢ Removable Flash memory or Flash drives uses solid state media.

<u>Tapes</u>

- ➢ In the past, **tapes** were the most popular storage option for backups because of their low cost.
- ➢ Tapes have various limitations in terms of performance and management, as listed below:
  - i. Data is stored on the tape linearly along the length of the tape. Search and retrieval of data are done sequentially, and it invariably takes several seconds to access the data. As a result, **random data access is slow and time-consuming**.
  - ii. In a shared computing environment, data stored on tape **cannot be accessed by multiple applications simultaneously**, restricting its use to one application at a time.
  - iii. On a tape drive, the read/write head touches the tape surface, so the tape degrades or wears out after repeated use.
  - iv. The storage and retrieval requirements of data from the tape and the overhead associated with managing the tape media are significant.
- ➢ Due to these limitations and availability of low-cost disk drives, tapes are no longer a preferred choice as a backup destination for enterprise-class data centers.

Optical Disc Storage:

- ➢ It is popular in small, single-user computing environments.
- ➢ It is frequently used by individuals to store photos or as a backup medium on personal or laptop computers.

- It is also used as a distribution medium for small applications, such as games, or as a means to transfer small amounts of data from one computer system to another.
- The capability to **write once and read many (WORM)** is one advantage of optical disc storage. Eg: CD-ROM
- Collections of optical discs in an array, called a **jukebox**, are still used as a fixed-content storage solution.
- Other forms of optical discs include CD-RW, Blu-ray disc, and other variations of DVD.

Disk Drives:
- **Disk drives** are the most popular storage medium used in modern computers for storing and accessing data for performance-intensive, online applications.
- Disks support rapid access to random data locations.
- Disks have large capacity.
- Disk storage arrays are configured with multiple disks to provide **increased capacity** and **enhanced performance**.
- Disk drives are accessed through predefined protocols, such as ATA, SATA, SAS, and FC.
- These protocols are implemented on the disk interface controllers.
- Disk interface controllers were earlier implemented as separate cards, which were connected to the motherboard.
- Modern disk interface controllers are integrated with the disk drives; therefore, disk drives are known by the protocol interface they support, for example SATA disk, FC disk, etc.

Data Protection: RAID

- In 1987, Patterson, Gibson, and Katz at the University of California, Berkeley, published a paper titled "A Case for **Redundant Arrays of Inexpensive Disks (RAID)**."
- **RAID is the use of small-capacity, inexpensive disk drives as an alternative to large-capacity drives common on mainframe computers.**
- Later RAID has been redefined to refer to *independent* disks to reflect advances in the storage technology.

1.10 RAID Implementation Methods

- ➢ The two methods of RAID implementation are:
    1. Hardware RAID.
    2. Software RAID.

1.10.1 Hardware RAID

- ➢ In hardware RAID implementations, a specialized hardware controller is implemented either on the *host* or on the *array*.
- ➢ **Controller card RAID** is a *host-based hardware RAID* implementation in which a specialized RAID controller is installed in the host, and disk drives are connected to it.
- ➢ Manufacturers also integrate RAID controllers on motherboards.
- ➢ A host-based RAID controller is not an efficient solution in a data center environment with a large number of hosts.
- ➢ The external RAID controller is an *array-based hardware RAID*.
- ➢ It acts as an interface between the host and disks.
- ➢ It presents storage volumes to the host, and the host manages these volumes as physical drives.
- ➢ The key functions of the RAID controllers are as follows:
    - ✓ Management and control of disk aggregations
    - ✓ Translation of I/O requests between logical disks and physical disks
    - ✓ Data regeneration in the event of disk failures

1.10.2 Software RAID

- ➢ **Software RAID** uses host-based software to provide RAID functions.
- ➢ It is implemented at the operating-system level and does not use a dedicated hardware controller to manage the RAID array.
- ➢ Advantages when compared to Hardware RAID:
    - ✓ cost
    - ✓ simplicity benefits

- ➢ Limitations:
    - ✓ **Performance**: Software RAID affects overall system performance. This is due to additional CPU cycles required to perform RAID calculations.
    - ✓ **Supported features**: Software RAID does not support all RAID levels.
    - ✓ **Operating system compatibility**: Software RAID is tied to the host operating system; hence, upgrades to software RAID or to the operating system should be validated for compatibility. This leads to inflexibility in the data-processing environment.

1.11 RAID Techniques

- ➢ There are three RAID techniques
    1. striping
    2. mirroring
    3. parity

1.11.1 Striping

- ➢ **Striping** is a technique to spread data across multiple drives (more than one) to use the drives in parallel.
- ➢ All the read-write heads work simultaneously, allowing more data to be processed in a shorter time and increasing performance, compared to reading and writing from a single disk.
- ➢ Within each disk in a RAID set, a **predefined number of contiguously addressable** disk blocks are defined as a **strip**.
- ➢ The set of aligned strips that spans across all the disks within the RAID set is called a **stripe**.
- ➢ Fig 1.11 shows physical and logical representations of a striped RAID set.

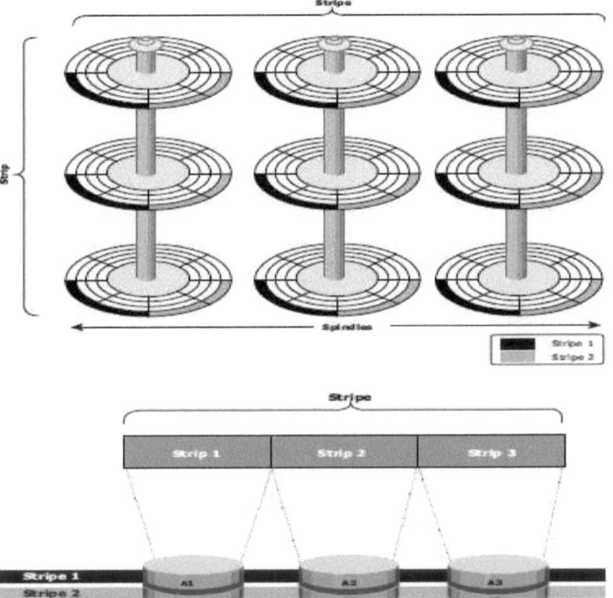

Fig 1.11: Striped RAID set

- **Strip size** (also called **stripe depth**) describes the number of blocks in a strip and is the maximum amount of data that can be written to or read from a single disk in the set.
- All strips in a stripe have the same number of blocks.
    - ✓ Having a smaller strip size means that data is broken into smaller pieces while spread across the disks.
- **Stripe size** is a multiple of strip size by the number of **data** disks in the RAID set.
    - ✓ Eg: In a 5 disk striped RAID set with a strip size of 64 KB, the stripe size is 320KB (64KB x 5).
- **Stripe width** refers to the number of *data* strips in a stripe.
- Striped RAID does not provide any data protection unless parity or mirroring is used.

1.11.2 Mirroring

➢ **Mirroring** is a technique whereby the same data is stored on two different disk drives, yielding two copies of the data.

➢ If one disk drive failure occurs, the data is intact on the surviving disk drive (see Fig 1.12) and the controller continues to service the host's data requests from the surviving disk of a mirrored pair.

➢ When the failed disk is replaced with a new disk, the controller copies the data from the surviving disk of the mirrored pair.

➢ This activity is transparent to the host.

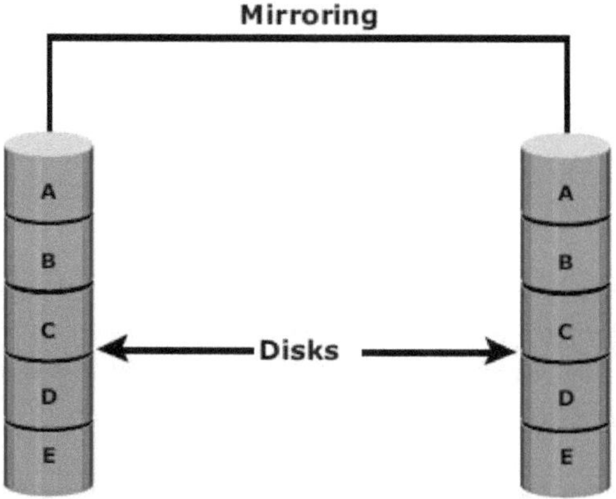

Fig 1.12: Mirrored disks in an array

➢ Advantages:
   ✓ complete data redundancy,
   ✓ mirroring enables fast recovery from disk failure.
   ✓ data protection

➢ Mirroring is not a substitute for data backup. Mirroring constantly captures changes in the data, whereas a backup captures point-in-time images of the data.

➢ Disadvantages:
   ✓ Mirroring involves duplication of data — the amount of storage capacity needed is

twice the amount of data being stored.

✓ Expensive

1.11.3 Parity

➤ **Parity** is a method to protect striped data from disk drive failure without the cost of mirroring.

➤ *An additional disk drive is added to hold parity*, a mathematical construct that allows re-creation of the missing data.

➤ Parity is a **redundancy technique** that ensures protection of data without maintaining a full set of duplicate data.

➤ Calculation of parity is a function of the RAID controller.

➤ Parity information can be stored on separate, dedicated disk drives or distributed across all the drives in a RAID set.

➤ Fig 1.13 shows a parity RAID set.

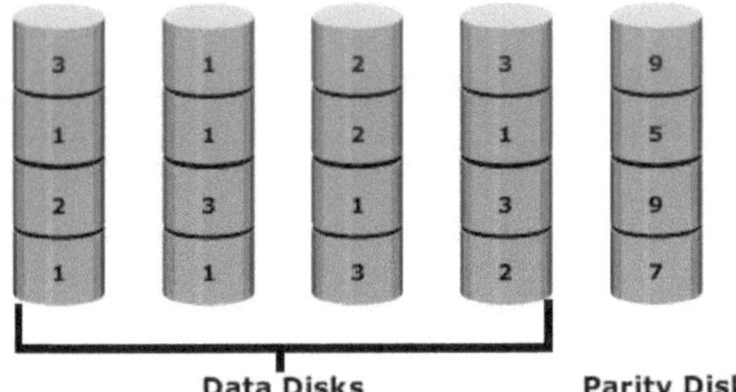

Fig 1.13: Parity RAID

➤ The first four disks, labeled *"Data Disks,"* contain the data. The fifth disk, labeled *"Parity Disk,"* stores the parity information, which, in this case, is the sum of the elements in each row.

➤ Now, if one of the data disks fails, the missing value can be calculated by subtracting the sum of the rest of the elements from the parity value.

➤ Here, computation of parity is represented as an arithmetic sum of the data. However, parity calculation is a bitwise XOR operation.

<u>XOR Operation:</u>

- ➤ A bit-by-bit Exclusive -OR (XOR) operation takes two bit patterns of equal length and performs the logical XOR operation on each pair of corresponding bits.
- ➤ The result in each position is 1 if the two bits are different, and 0 if they are the same.

- ➤ The truth table of the XOR operation is shown below (A and B denote inputs and C, the output the XOR operation).

Table 1.1: Truth table for XOR Operation

A	B	C
0	0	0
0	1	1
1	0	1
1	1	0

- ➤ If any of the data from A, B, or C is lost, it can be reproduced by performing an XOR operation on the remaining available data.
- ➤ Eg: if a disk containing all the data from A fails, the data can be regenerated by performing an XOR between B and C.
- ➤ Advantages:
    - ✓ Compared to mirroring, parity implementation considerably reduces the **cost** associated with data protection.
- ➤ Disadvantages:
    - ✓ Parity information is generated from data on the data disk. Therefore, parity is recalculated every time there is a change in data.
    - ✓ This recalculation is time-consuming and affects the performance of the RAID array.
- ➤ For parity RAID, the stripe size calculation does not include the parity strip.
- ➤ Eg: in a five (4 + 1) disk parity RAID set with a strip size of 64 KB, the stripe size will be 256 KB (64 KB x 4).

1.12 RAID Levels

- ➢ RAID Level selection is determined by below factors:
    - ✓ Application performance
    - ✓ data availability requirements
    - ✓ cost
- ➢ RAID Levels are defined on the basis of:
    - ✓ Striping
    - ✓ Mirroring
    - ✓ Parity techniques
- ➢ Some RAID levels use a single technique whereas others use a combination of techniques.
- ➢ Table 1.2 shows the commonly used RAID levels

Table 1.2: RAID Levels

LEVELS	BRIEF DESCRIPTION
RAID 0	Striped set with no fault tolerance
RAID 1	Disk mirroring
Nested	Combinations of RAID levels. Example: RAID 1 + RAID 0
RAID 3	Striped set with parallel access and a dedicated parity disk
RAID 4	Striped set with independent disk access and a dedicated parity disk
RAID 5	Striped set with independent disk access and distributed parity
RAID 6	Striped set with independent disk access and dual distributed parity

1.12.1 RAID 0

- ➢ **RAID 0** configuration uses *data striping techniques*, where data is striped across all the disks within a RAID set. Therefore it utilizes the full storage capacity of a RAID set.
- ➢ To read data, all the strips are put back together by the controller.
- ➢ Fig 1.14 shows RAID 0 in an array in which data is striped across five disks.

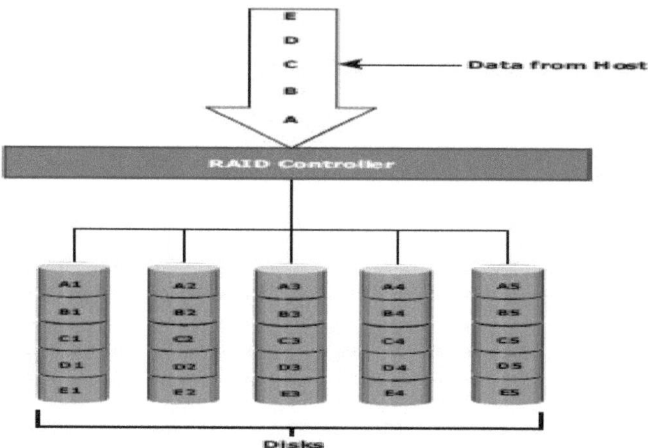

Fig 1.14: RAID 0

- When the number of drives in the RAID set increases, performance improves because more data can be read or written simultaneously.
- RAID 0 is a good option for applications that need high I/O throughput.
- However, if these applications require high availability during drive failures, RAID 0 does not provide data protection and availability.

1.12.2 RAID 1

- **RAID 1** is based on the *mirroring* technique.
- In this RAID configuration, data is mirrored to provide *fault tolerance* (see Fig 1.15). A
- RAID 1 set consists of two disk drives and every write is written to both disks.
- The mirroring is transparent to the host.
- During disk failure, the impact on data recovery in RAID 1 is the least among all RAID implementations. This is because the RAID controller uses the mirror drive for data recovery.
- RAID 1 is suitable for applications that require high availability and cost is no constraint.

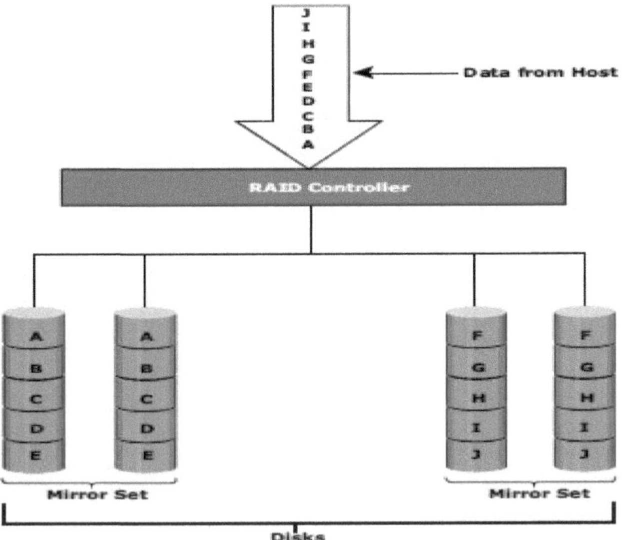

Fig 1.15: RAID 1

1.12.3 Nested RAID

➢ Most data centers require data redundancy and performance from their RAID arrays.

➢ RAID 1+0 and RAID 0+1 combine the performance benefits of RAID 0 with the redundancy benefits of RAID 1.

➢ They use striping and mirroring techniques and combine their benefits.

➢ These types of RAID require an even number of disks, the minimum being four (see Fig 1.16).

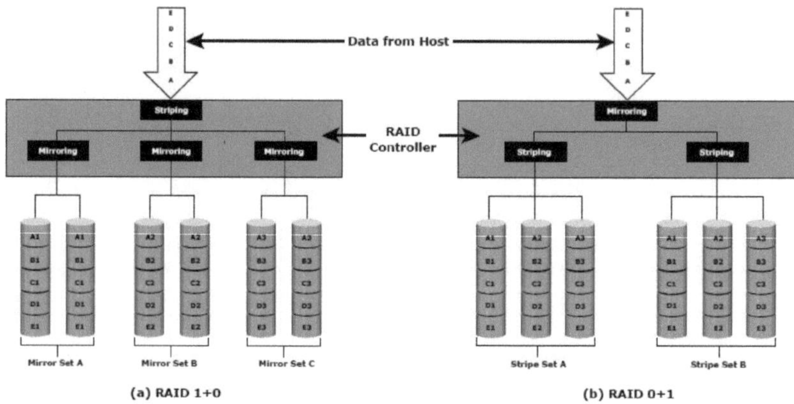

Fig 1.16: Nested RAID

RAID 1+0:

➢ RAID 1+0 is also known as RAID 10 (Ten) or RAID 1/0.

➢ RAID 1+0 performs well for workloads with small, random, write-intensive I/Os.

➢ Some applications that benefit from RAID 1+0 include the following:

  ✓ High transaction rate Online Transaction Processing (OLTP)

  ✓ Large messaging installations

  ✓ Database applications with write intensive random access workloads

➢ **RAID 1+0** is also called striped mirror.

➢ The basic element of RAID 1+0 is a mirrored pair, which means that data is first mirrored and then both copies of the data are striped across multiple disk drive pairs in a RAID set.

➢ When replacing a failed drive, only the mirror is rebuilt. The disk array controller uses the surviving drive in the mirrored pair for data recovery and continuous operation.

Working of RAID 1+0:

➢ Eg: consider an example of six disks forming a RAID 1+0 (RAID 1 first and then RAID 0) set.

➢ These six disks are paired into three sets of two disks, where each set acts as a RAID 1 set (mirrored pair of disks). Data is then striped across all the three mirrored sets to form RAID 0.

- ➤ Following are the steps performed in RAID 1+0 (see Fig 1.16 [a]):
    - ✓ Drives 1+2 = RAID 1 (Mirror Set A)
    - ✓ Drives 3+4 = RAID 1 (Mirror Set B)
    - ✓ Drives 5+6 = RAID 1 (Mirror Set C)
- ➤ Now, RAID 0 striping is performed across sets A through C.
- ➤ In this configuration, if drive 5 fails, then the mirror set C alone is affected. It still has drive 6 and continues to function and the entire RAID 1+0 array also keeps functioning.
- ➤ Now, suppose drive 3 fails while drive 5 was being replaced. In this case the array still continues to function because drive 3 is in a different mirror set.
- ➤ So, in this configuration, up to three drives can fail without affecting the array, as long as they are all in different mirror sets.
- ➤ **RAID 0+1** is also called a mirrored stripe.
- ➤ The basic element of RAID 0+1 is a stripe. This means that the process of striping data across disk drives is performed initially, and then the entire stripe is mirrored.
- ➤ In this configuration if one drive fails, then the entire stripe is faulted.

  <u>Working of RAID 0+1:</u>
- ➤ Eg: Consider the same example of six disks forming a RAID 0+1 (that is, RAID 0 first and then RAID 1).
- ➤ Here, six disks are paired into two sets of three disks each.
- ➤ Each of these sets, in turn, act as a RAID 0 set that contains three disks and then these two sets are mirrored to form RAID 1.
- ➤ Following are the steps performed in RAID 0+1 (see Fig 1.16 [b]):
    - ✓ Drives 1 + 2 + 3 = RAID 0 (Stripe Set A)
    - ✓ Drives 4 + 5 + 6 = RAID 0 (Stripe Set B)
- ➤ These two stripe sets are mirrored.
- ➤ If one of the drives, say drive 3, fails, the entire stripe set A fails.
- ➤ A rebuild operation copies the entire stripe, copying the data from each disk in the healthy stripe to an equivalent disk in the failed stripe.
- ➤ This causes increased and unnecessary I/O load on the surviving disks and makes the RAID set more vulnerable to a second disk failure.

1.12.4 RAID 3

- RAID 3 stripes data for high performance and uses parity for improved fault tolerance.
- Parity information is stored on a dedicated drive so that data can be reconstructed if a drive fails. For example, of five disks, four are used for data and one is used for parity.
- RAID 3 always reads and writes complete stripes of data across all disks, as the drives operate in parallel. There are no partial writes that update one out of many strips in a stripe.
- RAID 3 provides good bandwidth for the transfer of large volumes of data. RAID 3 is used in applications that involve large sequential data access, such as video streaming.
- Fig 1.17 shows the RAID 3 implementation

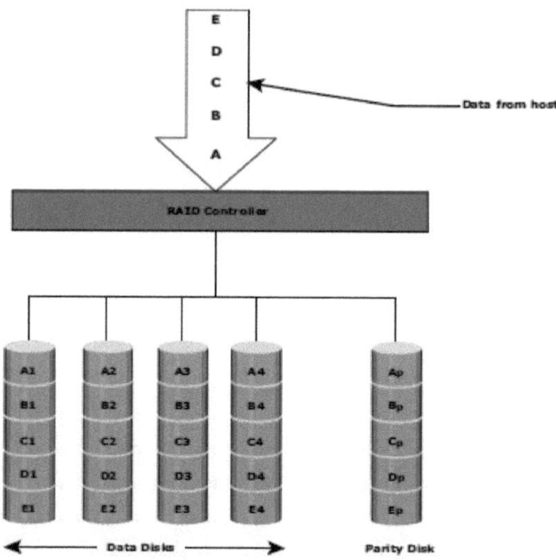

Fig 1.17: RAID 3

1.12.5 RAID 4

- RAID 4 stripes data for high performance and uses parity for improved fault tolerance. Data is striped across all disks except the parity disk in the array.
- Parity information is stored on a dedicated disk so that the data can be rebuilt if a drive fails. Striping is done at the block level.

➢ Unlike RAID 3, data disks in RAID 4 can be accessed independently so that specific data elements can be read or written on single disk without read or write of an entire stripe. RAID 4 provides good read throughput and reasonable write throughput.

1.12.6 RAID 5

➢ RAID 5 is a versatile RAID implementation.

➢ It is similar to RAID 4 because it uses striping. The drives (strips) are also independently accessible.

➢ The difference between RAID 4 and RAID 5 is the parity location. In RAID 4, parity is written to a dedicated drive, creating a write bottleneck for the parity disk

➢ In RAID 5, parity is distributed across all disks. The distribution of parity in RAID 5 overcomes the Write bottleneck. Below Figure illustrates the RAID 5 implementation.

➢ Fig 1.18 illustrates the RAID 5 implementation.

➢ RAID 5 is good for random, read-intensive I/O applications and preferred for messaging, data mining, medium-performance media serving, and relational database management system (RDBMS) implementations, in which database administrators (DBAs) optimize data access.

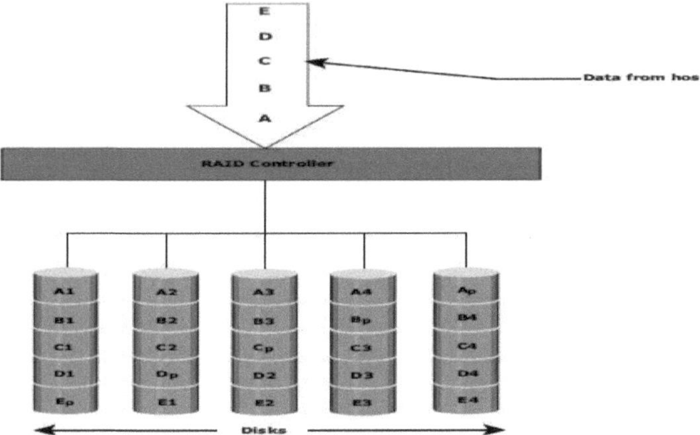

Fig 1.18: RAID 5

1.12.7 RAID 6

- ➤ RAID 6 includes a second parity element to enable survival in the event of the failure of two disks in a RAID group. Therefore, a RAID 6 implementation requires at least four disks.
- ➤ RAID 6 distributes the parity across all the disks. The write penalty in RAID 6 is more than that in RAID 5; therefore, RAID 5 writes perform better than RAID 6. The rebuild operation in RAID 6 may take longer than that in RAID 5 due to the presence of two parity sets.
- ➤ Fig 1.19 illustrates the RAID 6 implementation

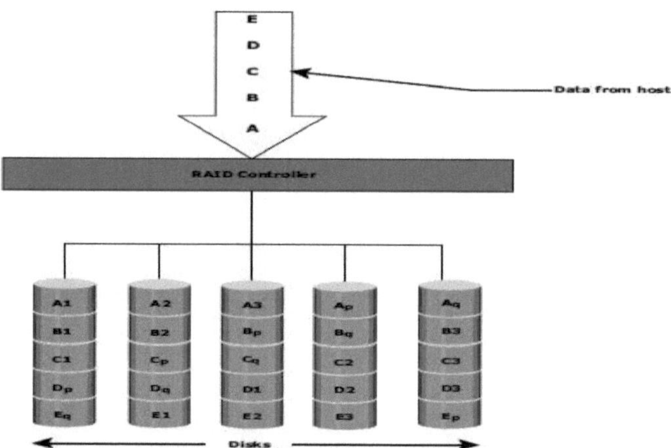

Fig 1.19: RAID 6

1.13 RAID Impact on Disk Performance

- ➤ When choosing a RAID type, it is imperative to consider its impact on disk performance and application IOPS.
- ➤ In both mirrored (RAID 1) and parity RAID (RAID 5) configurations, every write operation translates into more I/O overhead for the disks which is referred to as **write penalty**.
- ➤ In a RAID 1 implementation, every write operation must be performed on two disks configured as a mirrored pair. **The write penalty is 2.**
- ➤ In a RAID 5 implementation, a write operation may manifest as four I/O operations. When performing small I/Os to a disk configured with RAID 5, the controller has to read, calculate, and write a parity segment for every data write operation.
- ➤ Fig 1.20 illustrates a single write operation on RAID 5 that contains a group of five disks.

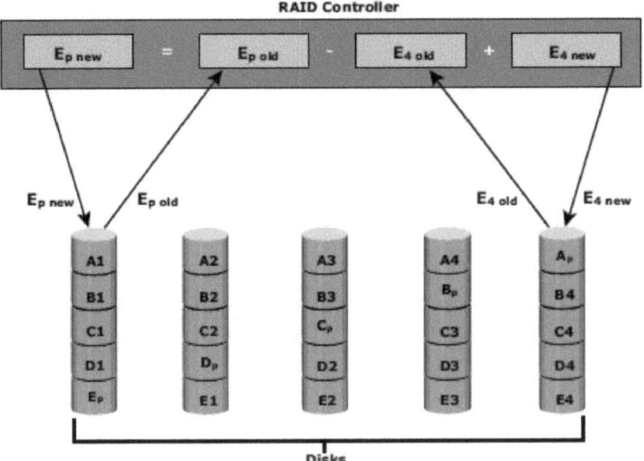

Fig 1.20: Write Penalty in RAID 5

➢ Four of these disks are used for data and one is used for parity.

➢ The **parity (E_p)** at the controller is calculated as follows:

$$E_p = E_1 + E_2 + E_3 + E_4 \ (XOR \ operations)$$

➢ Whenever the controller performs a write I/O, parity must be computed by reading the old parity (E_p old) and the old data (E_4 old) from the disk, which means two read I/Os.

➢ The new parity (E_p new) is computed as follows:

$$E_p \ new = E_p \ old - E_4 \ old + E_4 \ new \ (XOR \ operations)$$

➢ After computing the new parity, the controller completes the write I/O by doing two write I/Os for the new data and the new parity onto the disks..

➢ Therefore, the controller performs two disk reads and two disk writes for every write operation, and **the write penalty is 4**.

➢ In RAID 6, which maintains dual parity, a disk write requires **three read operations**: two parity and one data.

➢ After calculating both new parities, the controller performs **three write operations**: two parity and an I/O.

➢ Therefore, in a RAID 6 implementation, the controller performs six I/O operations for each write I/O, and the **write penalty is 6**.

1.14 Components of an Intelligent Storage System

➢ Intelligent Storage Systems are **feature-rich RAID arrays** that provide highly optimized I/O processing capabilities.

➢ These storage systems are configured with a large amount of memory (called *cache*) and multiple I/O paths and use sophisticated algorithms to meet the requirements of performance-sensitive applications.

➢ An intelligent storage system consists of **four key components** (Refer Fig 1.21):

- ✓ Front End
- ✓ Cache
- ✓ Back end
- ✓ Physical disks.

➢ An I/O request received from the host at the front-end port is processed through cache and the back end, to enable storage and retrieval of data from the physical disk.

➢ A read request can be serviced directly from cache if the requested data is found in cache.

➢ In modern intelligent storage systems, front end, cache, and back end are typically integrated on a single board (referred to as a storage processor or storage controller).

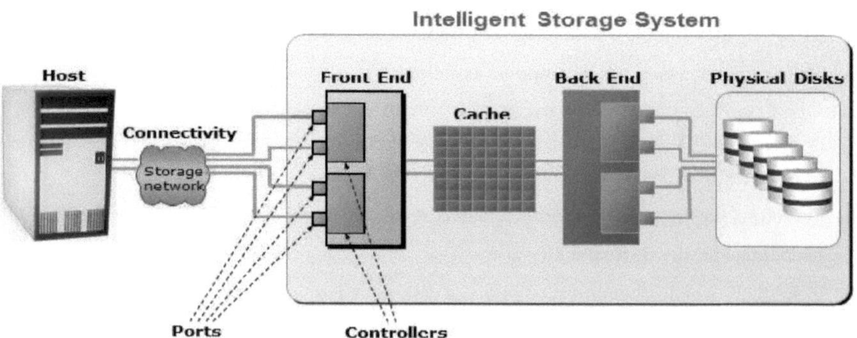

Fig 1.21 Components of an Intelligent Storage System

1.14.1 Front End

➢ The front end provides the interface between the storage system and the host.

➢ It consists of two components:

- i. Front-End Ports
- ii. Front-End Controllers.

- ➤ A front end has redundant controllers for high availability, and each controller contains multiple **front-end ports** that enable large numbers of hosts to connect to the intelligent storage system.
- ➤ Each front-end controller has processing logic that executes the appropriate transport protocol, such as Fibre Channel, iSCSI, FICON, or FCoE for storage connections.
- ➤ **Front-end controllers** route data to and from cache via the internal data bus.
- ➤ When the cache receives the write data, the controller sends an acknowledgment message back to the host.

1.14.2 Cache

- ➤ **Cache** is semiconductor memory where data is placed temporarily to reduce the time required to service I/O requests from the host.
- ➤ Cache improves storage system **performance** by isolating hosts from the mechanical delays associated with rotating disks or hard disk drives (HDD).
- ➤ Rotating disks are the slowest component of an intelligent storage system. Data access on rotating disks usually takes several millisecond because of seek time and rotational latency.
- ➤ **Accessing data from cache is fast and typically takes less than a millisecond**.
- ➤ On intelligent arrays, write data is first placed in cache and then written to disk.

Structure Of Cache

- ➤ Cache is organized into pages, which is the smallest unit of cache allocation. The size of a cache page is configured according to the application I/O size.
- ➤ Cache consists of the **data store** and **tag RAM**.
- ➤ The data store holds the data whereas the tag RAM tracks the location of the data in the data store (see Fig 1.22) and in the disk.
- ➤ Entries in tag RAM indicate where data is found in cache and where the data belongs on the disk.
- ➤ Tag RAM includes a dirty bit flag, which indicates whether the data in cache has been committed to the disk.
- ➤ It also contains time-based information, such as the time of last access, which is used to identify cached information that has not been accessed for a long period and may be freed up.

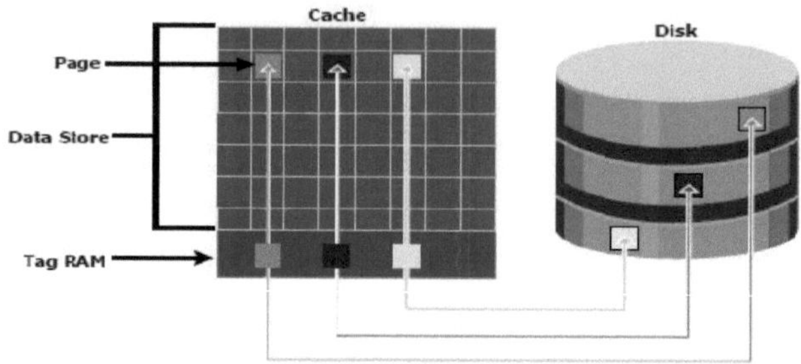

Fig 1.22: Structure of cache

Read Operation with Cache

- When a host issues a read request, the storage controller reads the tag RAM to determine whether the required data is available in cache.

- If the requested data is found in the cache, it is called a **read cache hit** or **read hit** and data is sent directly to the host, without any disk operation (see Fig 1.23[a]).This provides a fast response time to the host (about a millisecond).

- If the requested data is not found in cache, it is called a **cache miss** and the data must be read from the disk. The back-end controller accesses the appropriate disk and retrieves the requested data. Data is then placed in cache and is finally sent to the host through the front- end controller.

- Cache misses increase I/O response time.

- A **Pre-fetch**, or **Read-ahead,** algorithm is used when read requests are sequential. In a sequential read request, a contiguous set of associated blocks is retrieved. Several other blocks that have not yet been requested by the host can be read from the disk and placed into cache in advance. When the host subsequently requests these blocks, the read operations will be read hits.

- This process significantly improves the response time experienced by the host.

- The intelligent storage system offers *fixed* and *variable prefetch sizes*.

- In **fixed pre-fetch**, the intelligent storage system pre-fetches a fixed amount of data. It is most suitable when I/O sizes are uniform.

- In **variable pre-fetch**, the storage system pre-fetches an amount of data in multiples of the size of the host request.

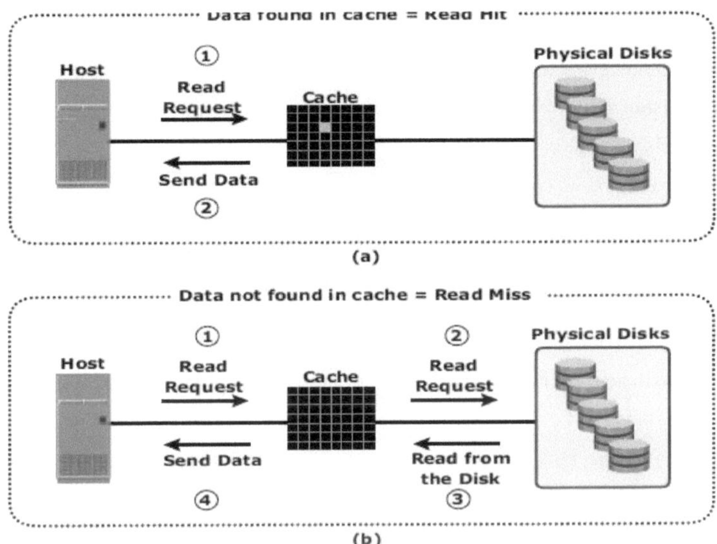

Fig 1.23 : Read hit and read miss

Write Operation with Cache

- ➤ Write operations with cache provide performance advantages over writing directly to disks.

- ➤ When an I/O is written to cache and acknowledged, it is completed in far less time (from the host's perspective) than it would take to write directly to disk.

- ➤ *Sequential writes* also offer opportunities for optimization because many smaller writes can be coalesced for larger transfers to disk drives with the use of cache.

- ➤ **A write operation** with cache is implemented in the following ways:

- ➤ **Write-back cache:** Data is placed in cache and an acknowledgment is sent to the host immediately. Later, data from several writes are committed to the disk. Write response times are much faster, as the write operations are isolated from the mechanical delays of the disk. However, uncommitted data is at risk of loss in the event of cache failures.

- ➤ **Write-through cache:** Data is placed in the cache and immediately written to the disk, and an acknowledgment is sent to the host. Because data is committed to disk as it arrives, the risks of data loss are low but write response time is longer because of the disk operations.

➢ Cache can be bypassed under certain conditions, such as large size write I/O.

➢ In this implementation, if the size of an I/O request exceeds the predefined size, called **write aside size**, writes are sent to the disk directly to reduce the impact of large writes consuming a large cache space.

➢ This is useful in an environment where cache resources are constrained and cache is required for small random I/Os.

Cache Implementation

➢ Cache can be implemented as either **dedicated cache** or **global cache**.

➢ With **dedicated cache**, separate sets of memory locations are reserved for reads and writes.

➢ In **global cache**, both reads and writes can use any of the available memory addresses.

➢ Cache management is more efficient in a global cache implementation because only one global set of addresses has to be managed.

➢ Global cache allows users to specify the percentages of cache available for reads and writes for cache management.

Cache Management

➢ Cache is a finite and expensive resource that needs proper management.

➢ Even though modern intelligent storage systems come with a large amount of cache, when all cache pages are filled, some pages have to be freed up to accommodate new data and avoid performance degradation.

➢ Various cache management algorithms are implemented in intelligent storage systems to proactively maintain a set of free pages and a list of pages that can be potentially freed up whenever required.

➢ The most commonly used algorithms are listed below:

    ✓ **Least Recently Used (LRU):** An algorithm that continuously monitors data access in cache and identifies the cache pages that have not been accessed for a long time. LRU either frees up these pages or marks them for reuse. This algorithm is based on the assumption that data which hasn't been accessed for a while will not be requested by the host.

✓ **Most Recently Used (MRU):** In MRU, the pages that have been accessed most recently are freed up or marked for reuse. This algorithm is based on the assumption that recently accessed data may not be required for a while

➤ As cache fills, the storage system must take action to **flush dirty pages** (data written into the cache but not yet written to the disk) to manage space availability.

➤ **Flushing** is the process that commits data from cache to the disk.

➤ On the basis of the I/O access rate and pattern, high and low levels called **watermarks** are set in cache to manage the flushing process.

➤ **High watermark (HWM)** is the cache utilization level at which the storage system starts high-speed flushing of cache data.

➤ **Low watermark (LWM)** is the point at which the storage system stops flushing data to the disks.

➤ The *cache utilization level*, as shown in Fig 1.24, drives the mode of flushing to be used:

✓ **Idle flushing:** Occurs continuously, at a modest rate, when the cache utilization level is between the high and low watermark.

✓ **High watermark flushing:** Activated when cache utilization hits the high watermark. The storage system dedicates some additional resources for flushing. This type of flushing has some impact on I/O processing.

✓ **Forced flushing:** Occurs in the event of a large I/O burst when cache reaches 100 percent of its capacity, which significantly affects the I/O response time. In forced flushing, system flushes the cache on priority by allocating more resources.

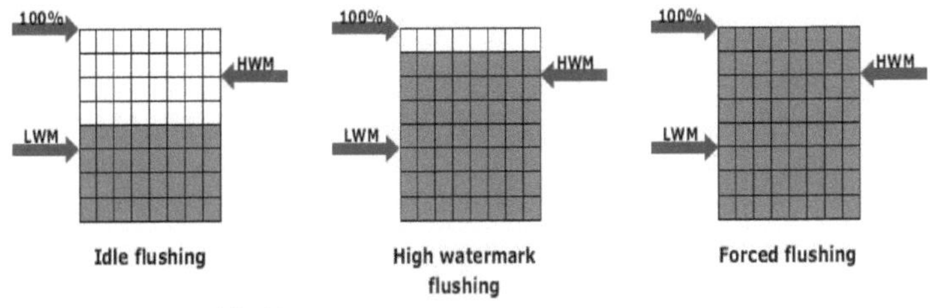

Fig 1.24 : Types of flushing

Cache Data Protection

➤ Cache is volatile memory, so a power failure or any kind of cache failure will cause loss of the data that is not yet committed to the disk.

- This risk of losing uncommitted data held in cache can be mitigated using
    - i. cache mirroring
    - ii. cache vaulting

- **Cache mirroring**
    - ✓ Each write to cache is held in two different memory locations on two independent memory cards. In the event of a cache failure, the write data will still be safe in the mirrored location and can be committed to the disk.
    - ✓ Reads are staged from the disk to the cache, therefore, in the event of a cache failure, the data can still be accessed from the disk.
    - ✓ In cache mirroring approaches, the problem of maintaining *cache coherency* is introduced.
    - ✓ Cache coherency means that data in two different cache locations must be identical at all times. It is the responsibility of the array operating environment to ensure coherency.

- **Cache vaulting**
    - ✓ The risk of data loss due to power failure can be addressed in various ways:
        - powering the memory with a battery until the AC power is restored
        - using battery power to write the cache content to the disk.
    - ✓ If an extended power failure occurs, using batteries is not a viable option.
    - ✓ This is because in intelligent storage systems, large amounts of data might need to be committed to numerous disks, and batteries might not provide power for sufficient time to write each piece of data to its intended disk.
    - ✓ Storage vendors use a set of physical disks to dump the contents of cache during power failure. This is called *cache vaulting* and the disks are called vault drives.
    - ✓ When power is restored, data from these disks is written back to write cache and then written to the intended disks.

1.14.3 Back End

- The **back end** provides an interface between cache and the physical disks.
- It consists of two components:
    - i. Back-end ports
    - ii. Back-end controllers.
- The back end controls data transfers between cache and the physical disks.
- From cache, data is sent to the back end and then routed to the destination disk.

- Physical disks are connected to *ports* on the back end.
- The *back end controller* communicates with the disks when performing reads and writes and also provides additional, but limited, temporary data storage.
- The algorithms implemented on back-end controllers provide error detection and correction, and also RAID functionality.
- For high data protection and high availability, storage systems are configured with dual controllers with multiple ports.

1.14.4 Physical Disk

- A physical disk stores data persistently.
- Physical disks are connected to the back-end storage controller and provide persistent data storage.
- Modern intelligent storage systems provide support to a variety of disk drives with different speeds and types, such as FC, SATA, SAS, and flash drives.
- They also support the use of a mix of flash, FC, or SATA within the same array.

1.15 Types of Intelligent Storage Systems

- An intelligent storage system is divided into following two categories:
    1. High-end storage systems
    2. Midrange storage systems
- High-end storage systems have been implemented with active-active configuration, whereas midrange storage systems have been implemented with active-passive configuration.
- The distinctions between these two implementations are becoming increasingly insignificant.

1.15.1 High-end Storage Systems

- High-end storage systems, referred to as **active-active arrays,** are generally aimed at large enterprises for centralizing corporate data. These arrays are designed with a large number of controllers and cache memory.
- An active-active array implies that the host can perform I/Os to its LUNs across any of the available paths (see Fig 1.25).

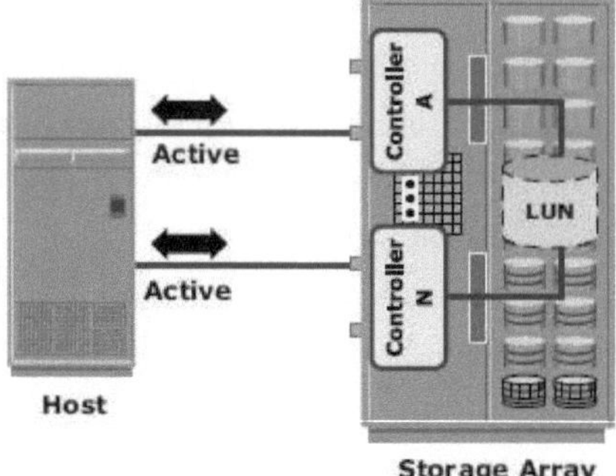

Fig 1.25 : Active-active configuration

Advantages of High-end storage:

➢ Large storage capacity

➢ Large amounts of cache to service host I/Os optimally

➢ Fault tolerance architecture to improve data availability

➢ Connectivity to mainframe computers and open systems hosts Availability of multiple front-end ports and interface protocols to serve a large number of hosts

➢ Availability of multiple back-end Fibre Channel or SCSI RAID controllers to manage disk processing

➢ Scalability to support increased connectivity, performance, and storage

➢ capacity requirements

➢ Ability to handle large amounts of concurrent I/Os from a number of servers and applications

➢ Support for array-based local and remote replication

1.15.2 Midrange Storage System

➢ Midrange storage systems are also referred to as **Active-Passive Arrays** and they are best suited for small- and medium-sized enterprises.

➢ They also provide optimal storage solutions at a *lower cost*.

➢ In an *active-passive* array, a host can perform I/Os to a LUN only through the paths to the **owning controller** of that LUN. These paths are called *Active Paths*. The other paths are *passive* with respect to this LUN.

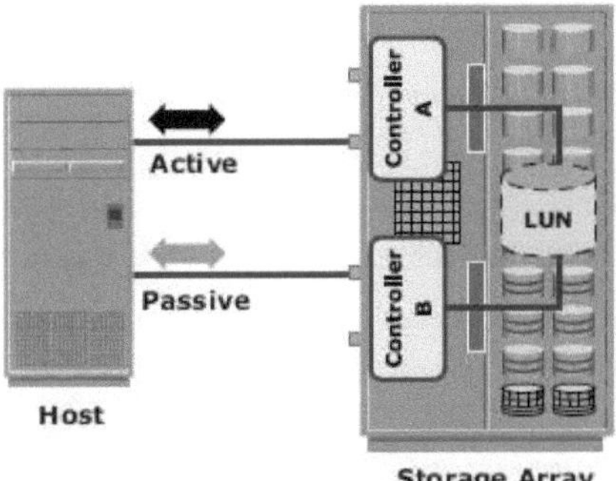

Fig 1.26 : Active-passive configuration

➢ As shown in Fig 1.26, the host can perform reads or writes to the LUN only through the path to controller A, as controller A is the owner of that LUN.

➢ The path to controller B remains **Passive** and no I/O activity is performed through this path.

➢ Midrange storage systems are typically designed with two controllers, each of which contains host interfaces, cache, RAID controllers, and disk drive interfaces.

➢ Midrange arrays are designed to meet the requirements of small and medium enterprise applications; therefore, they host less storage capacity and cache than high-end storage arrays.

➢ There are also fewer front-end ports for connection to hosts.

➢ But they ensure high redundancy and high performance for applications with predictable workloads.

➢ They also support array-based local and remote replication.

1.16 Virtual Storage Provisioning

➢ **Virtual provisioning** enables creating and presenting a LUN with more capacity than is physically allocated to it on the storage array.

➢ The LUN created using virtual provisioning is called a *thin LUN* to distinguish it from the traditional LUN.

➢ Thin LUNs do not require physical storage to be completely allocated to them at the time they are created and presented to a host.

➢ Physical storage is allocated to the host *"on-demand"* from a *shared pool* of physical capacity.

- ➤ A *shared pool* consists of physical disks.

- ➤ A shared pool in virtual provisioning is analogous to a *RAID group*, which is a collection of drives on which LUNs are created.

- ➤ Similar to a RAID group, a shared pool supports a single RAID protection level. However, unlike a RAID group, a shared pool might contain large numbers of drives.

- ➤ Shared pools can be homogeneous (containing a single drive type) or heterogeneous (containing mixed drive types, such as flash, FC, SAS, and SATA drives).

- ➤ Virtual provisioning enables more efficient allocation of storage to hosts.

- ➤ Virtual provisioning also enables oversubscription, where more capacity is presented to the hosts than is actually available on the storage array.

- ➤ Both shared pool and thin LUN can be expanded non-disruptively as the storage requirements of the hosts grow.

- ➤ Multiple shared pools can be created within a storage array, and a shared pool may be shared by multiple thin LUNs.

- ➤ Fig 1.27 illustrates the provisioning of thin LUNs.

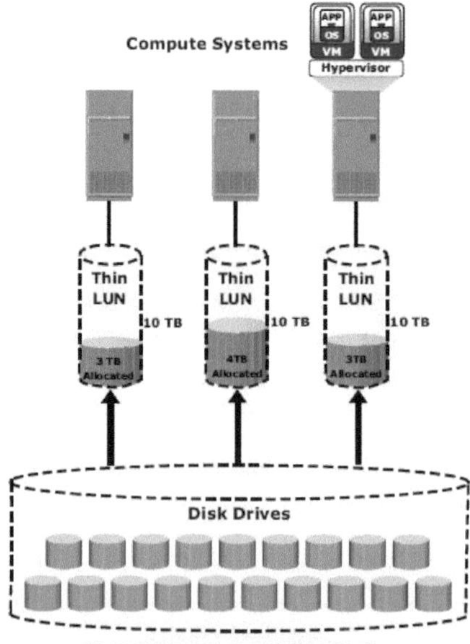

Fig 1.27: Virtual Provisioning

Comparison between Virtual and Traditional Storage Provisioning

➤ Virtual provisioning improves storage capacity utilization and simplifies storage management.

➤ Figure 1.28 shows an example, comparing virtual provisioning with traditional storage provisioning.

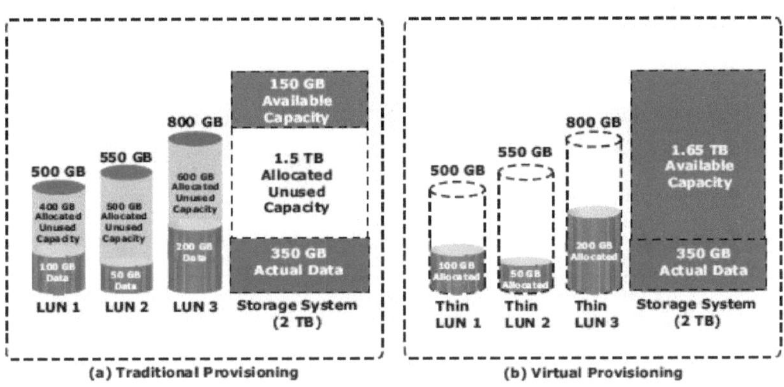

hosts (see Fig 1.28 [a]). The total storage capacity of the storage system is 2 TB.

➤ The allocated capacity of LUN 1 is 500 GB, of which only 100 GB is consumed, and the remaining 400 GB is unused. The size of LUN 2 is 550 GB, of which 50 GB is consumed, and 500 GB is unused. The size of LUN 3 is 800 GB, of which 200 GB is consumed, and 600 GB is unused.

➤ In total, the storage system has 350 GB of data, 1.5 TB of allocated but unused capacity, and only 150 GB of remaining capacity available for other applications.

➤ Now consider the same 2 TB storage system with **virtual provisioning** (see Fig 1.28 [b]).

➤ Here, three *thin LUNs* of the same sizes are created. However, there is no allocated unused capacity.

➤ **In total, the storage system with virtual provisioning has the same 350 GB of data, but 1.65 TB of capacity is available for other applications, whereas only 150 GB is available in traditional storage provisioning.**

STORAGE NETWORKING TECHNOLOGIES AND VIRTUALIZATION

SAN is a high-speed dedicated network of servers and shared storage. Commom SAN deployments are:
- ✓ FC SAN
- ✓ IP SAN

2.1 Fibre Channel: Overview

- ➤ The FC architecture forms the fundamental construct of the SAN infrastructure.

- ➤ **Fibre Channel** is a high-speed network technology that runs on high-speed optical fiber cables (preferred for front-end SAN connectivity) and serial copper cables (preferred for back-end disk connectivity).

- ➤ The FC technology was created to meet the demand for increased speeds of data transfer among computers, servers, and mass storage subsystems.

2.2 Components of SAN

- ➤ Components of FC SAN infrastructure are:
1) **Node Ports,**
2) **Cabling,**
3) **Connectors,**
4) **Interconnecting Devices (Such As Fc Switches Or Hubs),**
5) **San Management Software.**

Node Ports

- ➤ In fibre channel, devices such as hosts, storage and tape libraries are all referred to as **Nodes.**

- ➤ Each node is a **source or destination** of information for one or more nodes.

- ➤ Each node requires one or more ports to provide a physical interface for communicating with other nodes.

- ➤ A port operates in full-duplex data transmission mode with a **transmit (Tx) link and a**

receive (Rx) link (see Fig 2.1).

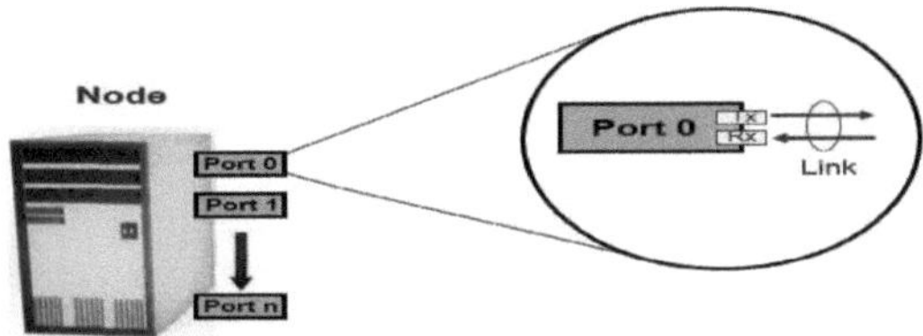

Fig 2.1: Nodes, Ports, links

Cabling

- ➢ SAN implementations use optical fiber cabling.
- ➢ Copper can be used for shorter distances for back-end connectivity
- ➢ Optical fiber cables carry data in the form of light.
- ➢ There are two types of optical cables :**Multi-Mode And Single-Mode.**

1) **Multi-mode fiber (MMF)** cable carries multiple beams of light projected at different angles simultaneously onto the core of the cable (see Fig 2.2 (a)).

   - ➢ In an MMF transmission, multiple light beams traveling inside the cable tend to disperse and collide. This collision weakens the signal strength after it travels a certain distance — a process known as *modal dispersion.*
   - ➢ MMFs are generally used within data centers for shorter distance runs

2) **Single-mode fiber (SMF)** carries a single ray of light projected at the center of the core (see Fig 2.2 (b)).

   - ➢ In an SMF transmission, a single light beam travels in a straight line through the core of the fiber.
   - ➢ The small core and the single light wave limits modal dispersion. Among all types of fibre cables, single-mode provides minimum signal attenuation over maximum distance (up to 10 km).
   - ➢ A single-mode cable is used for long-distance cable runs, limited only by the power

of the laser at the transmitter and sensitivity of the receiver.

➢ SMFs are used for longer distances.

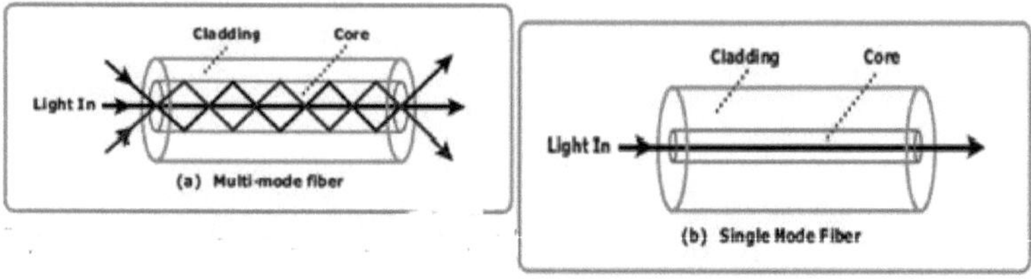

Fig 2.2: Multimode fiber and single-mode fiber

Connectors

➢ They are attached at the end of the cable to enable swift connection and disconnection of the cable to and from a port.

➢ A **Standard connector (SC)** (see Fig 2.3 (a)) and a **Lucent connector (LC)** (see Fig 2.3 (b)) are two commonly used connectors for fiber optic cables.

➢ An SC is used for data transmission speeds up to 1 Gb/s, whereas an LC is used for speeds up to 4 Gb/s.

➢ Figure 2.3 depicts a Lucent connector and a Standard connector.

➢ A Straight Tip (ST) is a fiber optic connector with a plug and a socket that is locked with a half-twisted bayonet lock (see Fig 2.3 (c)).

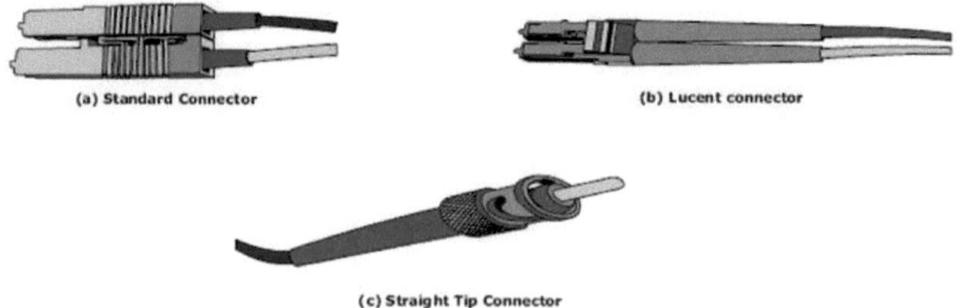

Fig 2.3: SC,LC, and ST connectors

Interconnect Devices

The commonly used interconnecting devices in SAN are

1) **Hubs,**
2) **Switches,**
3) **Directors**

- ➤ **Hubs** are used as communication devices in FC-AL implementations. Hubs physically connect nodes in a logical loop or a physical star topology.
- ➤ All the nodes must share the bandwidth because data travels through all the connection points. Because of availability of low cost and high performance switches, hubs are no longer used in SANs.
- ➤ **Switches** are more **intelligent** than hubs and directly **route data from one physical port to another**. Therefore, nodes do not share the bandwidth. Instead, each node has a dedicated communication path, resulting in bandwidth aggregation.
- ➤ Switches are available with:
    - ✓ Fixed port count
    - ✓ Modular design : port count is increased by installing additional port cards to open slots.
- ➤ **Directors are larger than switches** and are deployed for data center implementations.
- ➤ The function of directors is similar to that of FC switches, but directors have higher port count and fault tolerance capabilities.
- ➤ Port card or blade has multiple ports for connecting nodes and other FC switches

SAN Management Software

- ➤ SAN management software manages the interfaces between hosts, interconnect devices, and storage arrays.
- ➤ The software provides a view of the SAN environment and enables management of various resources from one central console.

➢ It provides key management functions, including mapping of storage devices, switches, and servers, monitoring and generating alerts for discovered devices, and logical partitioning of the SAN, called *zoning*

2.3 FC Connectivity

The FC architecture supports three basic interconnectivity options:

1) **Point-To-point,**
2) **Arbitrated Loop (Fc-AL),**
3) **FC Switched Fabric**

Point-to-Point

➢ **Point-to-point** is the simplest FC configuration — two devices are connected directly to each other, as shown in Fig 2.4.

➢ This configuration provides a dedicated connection for data transmission between nodes.

➢ The point-to-point configuration offers limited connectivity, as only two devices can communicate with each other at a given time.

➢ It cannot be scaled to accommodate a large number of network devices. Standard DAS uses point to- point connectivity.

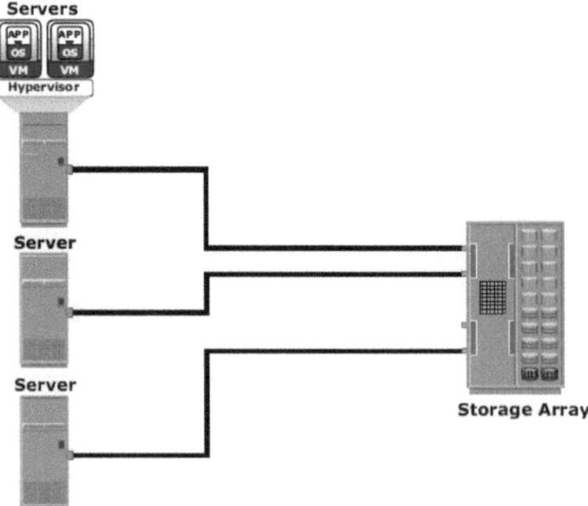

Fig 2.4: Point-to-point connectivity

Fibre Channel Arbitrated Loop

- ➢ In the FC-AL configuration, devices are attached to a shared loop, as shown in Fig 2.5.
- ➢ FC-AL has the characteristics of a **token ring topology and a physical star topology**.
- ➢ In FC-AL, each device contends with other devices to perform I/O operations. Devices on the loop must "arbitrate" to gain control of the loop.
- ➢ At any given time, only one device can perform I/O operations on the loop.
- ➢ FC-AL implementations may also use hubs whereby the arbitrated loop is physically connected in a star topology.

The FC-AL configuration has the following limitations in terms of scalability:

- ➢ FC-AL shares the bandwidth in the loop.
- ➢ Only one device can perform I/O operations at a time. Because each device in a loop has to wait for its turn to process an I/O request, the speed of data transmission is low in an FC-AL topology.
- ➢ FC-AL uses 8-bit addressing. It can support up to 127 devices on a loop.
- ➢ Adding or removing a device results in loop re-initialization, which can cause a momentary pause in loop traffic.

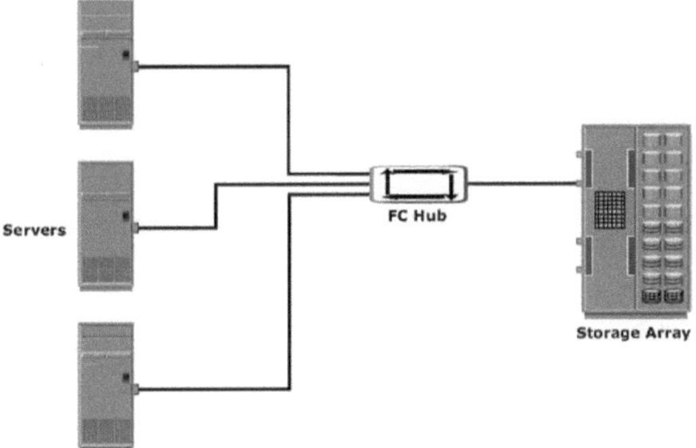

Fig 2.5: Fibre Channel Arbitrated Loop

Fibre Channel Switched Fabric(FC-SW)

- ➤ FC-SW provides dedicated data path and scalability.
- ➤ The addition and removal of a device doesnot affect the on-going traffic between other devices.
- ➤ FC-SW is referred to as **Fabric connect**.
- ➤ A Fabric is a logical space in which all nodes communicate with one another in a network. This virtual space can be created with a switch or a network of switches.
- ➤ Each switch in a fabric contains a a unique domain identifi er, which is part of the fabric's addressing scheme.
- ➤ In a switched fabric, the link between any two switches is called an *Interswitch link* (ISL).
- ➤ ISLs enable switches to be connected together to form a single, larger fabric.
- ➤ ISLs are used to transfer host-to-storage data and fabric management traffic from one switch to another.
- ➤ By using ISLs, a switched fabric can be expanded to connect a large number of nodes.

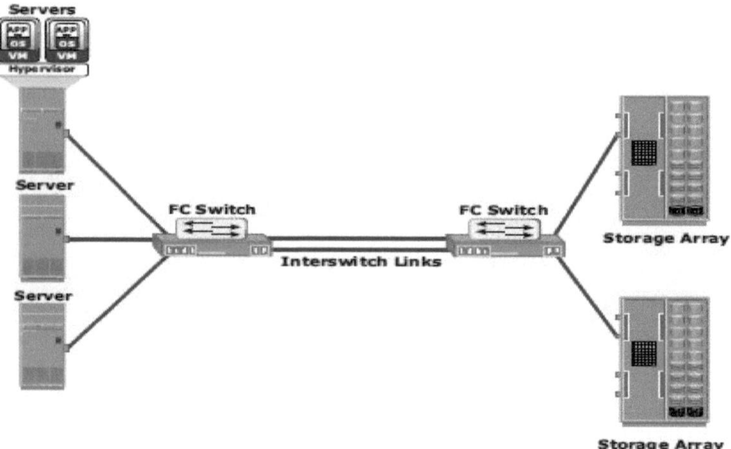

Fig 2.6: Fibre Channel switched Fabric

➢ A Fabric may contain tiers.

➢ The number of tiers in a fabric is based on the number of switches between two points that are farthest from each other

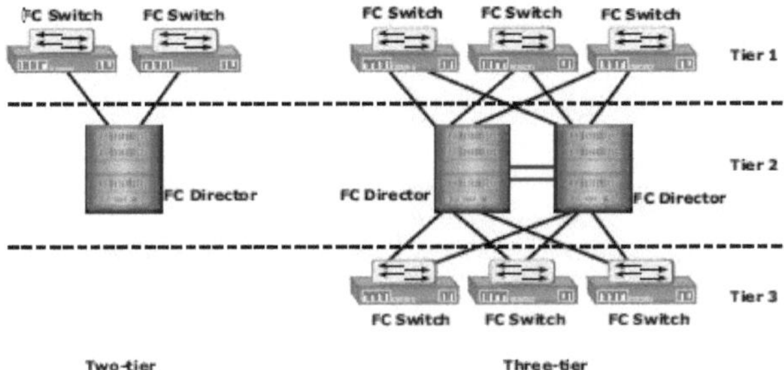

Fig 2.7: Tiered structure of Fibre Channel switched Fabric

FC-SW Transmission

➢ FC-SW uses switches that can switch data traffi c between nodes directly through switch ports.

➢ Frames are routed between source and destination by the fabric.

Node A want to communicate with Node B

① High priority initiator, Node A inserts the ARB frame in the loop.

② ARB frame is passed to the next node (Node D) in the loop.

③ Node D receives high priority ARB, therefore remains idle.

④ ARB is forwarded to next node (Node C) in the loop.

⑤ Node C receives high priority ARB, therefore remains idle.

⑥ ARB is forwarded to next node (Node B) in the loop.

⑦ Node B receives high priority ARB, therefore remains idle and

⑧ ARB is forwarded to next node (Node A) in the loop.

⑨ Node A receives ARB back; now it gains control of the loop and can start communicating with target Node B.

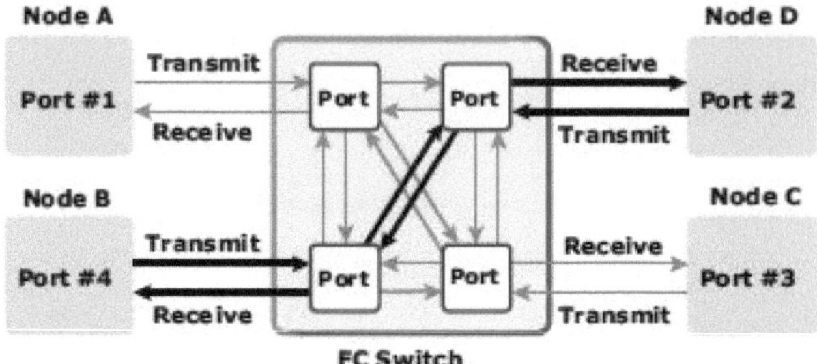

Fig 2.8: Data transmission in fibre channel switched fabric

2.4 Fibre Channel Architecture

- ➤ Connections in a SAN are accomplished using FC.
- ➤ ***Fibre Channel Protocol (FCP)* is the implementation of serial SCSI-3 over an FC network.** In the FCP architecture, all external and remote storage devices attached to the SAN appear as local devices to the host operating system.
- ➤ The key advantages of FCP are as follows:
    - ➤ Sustained transmission bandwidth over long distances.
    - ➤ Support for a larger number of addressable devices over a network.
    - ➤ Theoretically, FC can support over 15 million device addresses on a network.
    - ➤ Exhibits the characteristics of channel transport and provides speeds up to 8.5 Gb/s (8 GFC).

Fibre Channel Protocol Stack

- ➤ It is easier to understand a communication protocol by viewing it as a structure of independent layers.
- ➤ FCP defines the communication protocol in five layers:FC-0 through FC-4 (except FC-3 layer, which is not implemented).
- ➤ In a layered communication model, the peer layers on each node talk to each other through defined protocols.
- ➤ Fig 2.9 illustrates the fibre channel protocol stack.

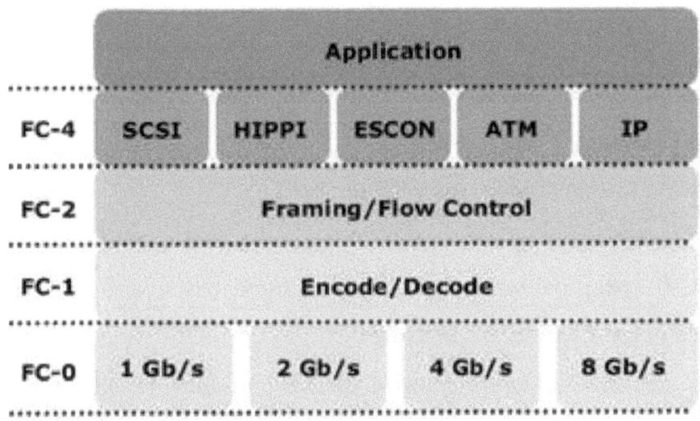

Fig 2.9: Fibre Channel Protocol Stack

> **FC-4 Upper Layer Protocol**

 ✓ FC-4 is the uppermost layer in the FCP stack.

 ✓ This layer defines the application interfaces and the way **Upper Layer Protocols (ULPs) are mapped to the lower FC layers.**

 ✓ The FC standard defines several protocols that can operate on the FC-4 layer (see Fig 2.9). Some of the protocols include SCSI, HIPPI Framing Protocol, Enterprise Storage Connectivity (ESCON), ATM, and IP.

> **FC-2 Transport Layer**

 ✓ The FC-2 is the transport layer that contains the payload, addresses of the source and destination ports, and link control information.

 ✓ The FC-2 layer provides Fibre Channel **addressing, structure, and organization of data (frames,sequences, and exchanges).** It also defines **fabric services, classes of service,flow control, and routing.**

> **FC-1 Transmission Protocol**

 ✓ This layer defines the transmission protocol that includes **serial encoding and decoding rules, special characters used, and error control.**

 ✓ At the transmitter node, an 8-bit character is encoded into a 10-bit transmissions character.

✓ This character is then transmitted to the receiver node.

✓ At the receiver node, the 10-bit character is passed to the FC-1 layer, which decodes the 10-bit character into the original 8-bit character.

➤ **FC-0 Physical Interface**

✓ FC-0 is the lowest layer in the FCP stack.

✓ This layer defines the physical interface, media, and transmission of raw bits.

✓ The FC-0 specification includes cables, connectors, and optical and electrical parameters for a variety of data rates.

✓ The FC transmission can use both electrical and optical media.

2.5 Fibre Channel Addressing

➤ An FC address is **dynamically assigned** when a port logs on to the fabric.

➤ The FC address has a distinct format, as shown in Fig 2.10. The addressing mechanism provided here corresponds to the fabric with the switch as an interconnecting device.

➤ The first field of the FC address contains the domain ID of the switch (see Fig 2.10).

➤ A *domain ID* is a unique number provided to each switch in the fabric.

➤ This is an 8-bit field, there are only 239 available addresses for domain ID because some addresses are deemed special and reserved for fabric management services.

➤ For example, FFFFFC is reserved for the name server, and FFFFFE is reserved for the fabric login service.

➤ The *area ID* is used to identify a group of switch ports used for connecting nodes. An example of a group of ports with a common area ID is a port card on the switch.

➤ The last field, the *port ID*, identifies the port within the group.

➤ The maximum possible number of node ports in a switched fabric is calculated as:
239 domains ¥ 256 areas ¥ 256 ports = 15,663,104

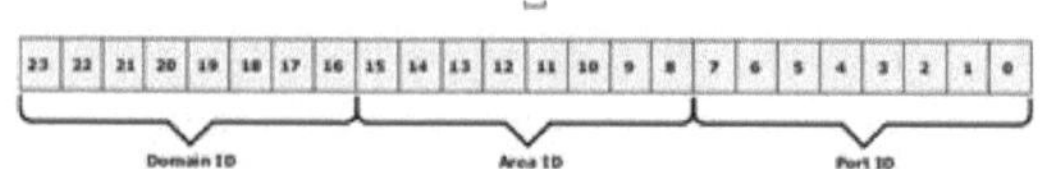

Fig 2.10 24 bit FC address of N_port

2.6 Zoning

- ➤ Zoning is an **FC switch function** that enables nodes within the fabric to be **logically segmented into groups** that can communicate with each other (see Fig 2.11).

- ➤ Whenever a change takes place in the name server database, the fabric controller sends a Registered State Change Notifi cation (RSCN) to all the nodes impacted by the change.

- ➤ If zoning is not configured, the fabric controller sends an RSCN to all the nodes in the fabric. Involving the nodes that are not impacted by the change results in increased fabric-management traffic.

- ➤ Zoning helps to limit the number of RSCNs in a fabric. In the presence of zoning, a fabric sends the RSCN to only those nodes in a zone where the change has occurred.

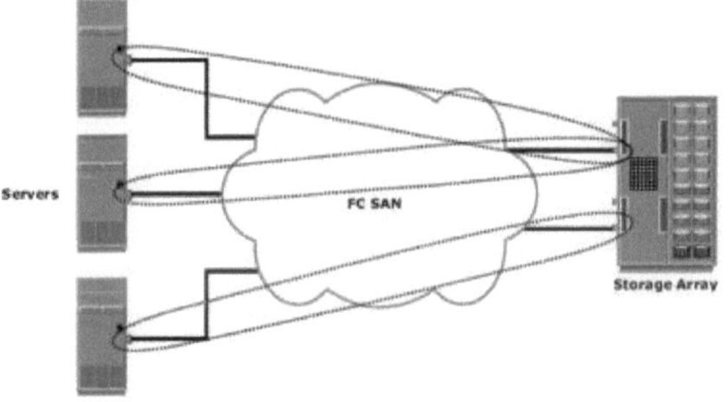

Fig 2.11 Zoning

- ➤ Multiple zone sets may be defined in a fabric, but only one zone set can be active at a time.
- ➤ A **zone set is a set of zones** and a **zone is a set of members**.
- ➤ A member may be in multiple zones. Members, zones, and zone sets form the hierarchy defined in the zoning process (see Fig 2.12).
- ➤ **Members** are nodes within the SAN that can be included in a zone.
- ➤ **Zones** comprise a set of members that have access to one another. A port or a node can be a member of multiple zones.
- ➤ **Zone sets** comprise a group of zones that can be activated or deactivated as a single entity in a fabric. Only one zone set per fabric can be active at a time.

> Zone sets are also referred to as *zone configurations*.

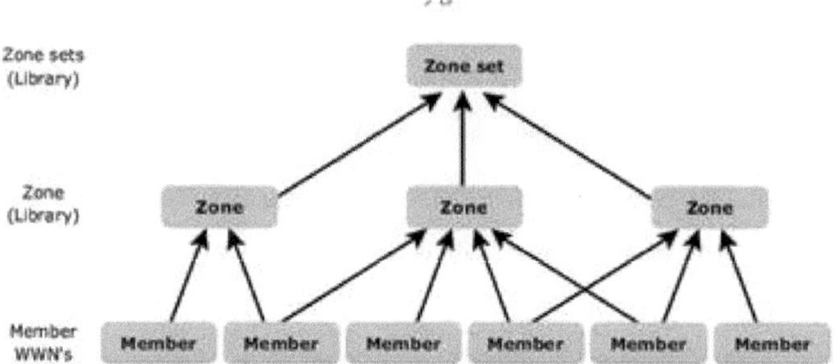

Fig 2.12: Members,Zones, and Zone sets

Types of Zoning

Zoning can be categorized into three types:

1) **Port zoning**
2) **WWN zoning**
3) **Mixed zoning**

Port zoning:

> It uses the **FC addresses** of the physical ports to define zones.

> In port zoning, access to data is determined by the physical switch port to which a node is connected.

> The **FC address is dynamically** assigned when the port logs on to the fabric. Therefore, any change in the fabric configuration affects zoning.

> Port zoning is also called **hard zoning.**

> Although this method is secure, it requires updating of zoning configuration information in the event of fabric reconfiguration.

WWN zoning:

> It uses World Wide Names to define zones.

> WWN zoning is also referred to as **soft zoning**.

➢ A major advantage of WWN zoning is its flexibility.

➢ It allows the SAN to be recabled without reconfiguring the zone information. This is possible because the WWN is static to the node port.

Mixed zoning:

➢ It combines the qualities of both WWN zoning and port zoning.

➢ Using mixed zoning enables a specific port to be tied to the WWN of a node.

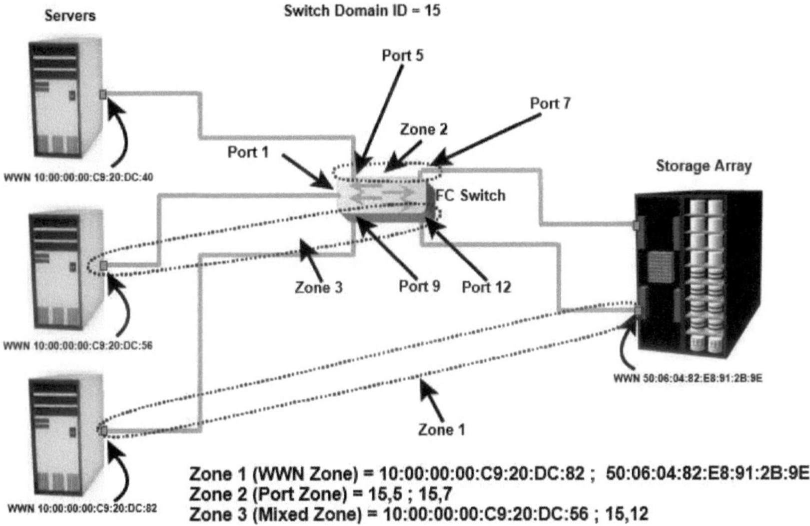

Fig 2.14: Types of Zoning

➢ Zoning is used in conjunction with LUN masking for controlling server access to storage. However, these are two different activities. Zoning takes place at the fabric level and LUN masking is done at the array level.

2.7 FC Topologies

> Fabric design follows standard topologies to connect devices. There are two types of topologies.

> > **Mesh Topology**
> > **Core-Edge Fabric**

Mesh Topology

> In a mesh topology, **each switch is directly connected to other switches by using ISLs.**

> This topology promotes enhanced connectivity within the SAN.

> When the number of ports on a network increases, the number of nodes that can participate and communicate also increases.

> A mesh topology may be one of the two types: **full mesh or partial mesh.**

> In a **full mesh, every switch is connected to every other switch** in the topology.

> Full mesh topology may be appropriate when the number of switches involved is small. A typical deployment would involve up to four switches or directors, with each of them servicing highly localized host-to-storage traffic. In a full mesh topology, a maximum of one ISL or hop is required for host-to-storage traffic.

> In a **partial mesh** topology, several hops or ISLs may be required for the traffic to reach its destination. Hosts and storage can be located anywhere in the fabric, and storage can be localized to a director or a switch in both mesh topologies. A full mesh topology with a symmetric design results in an even number of switches, whereas a partial mesh has an asymmetric design and may result in an odd number of switches. Fig 2.15 depicts both a full mesh and a partial mesh topology.

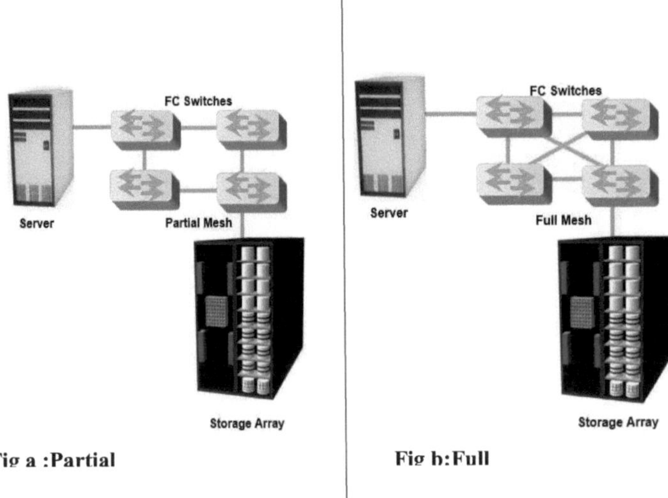

Fig a :Partial   Fig b:Full

Fig 2.15: Partial and Full mesh Topologies

Core-Edge Fabric

- In the **core-edge fabric** topology, there are two types of switch tiers in this fabric.
- The **edge tier** usually comprises switches and offers an inexpensive approach to adding more hosts in a fabric. The tier at the edge fans out from the tier at the core. The nodes on the edge can communicate with each other.
- The **core tier** usually comprises **enterprise directors** that ensure high fabric availability. Additionally all traffic has to either traverse through or terminate at this tier.
- In a two-tier configuration, all storage devices are connected to the core tier, facilitating fan-out.
- The host-to-storage traffic has to traverse one and two ISLs in a two-tier and three-tier configuration, respectively.
- The core-edge fabric topology increases connectivity within the SAN while conserving overall port utilization. If expansion is required, an additional edge switch can be connected to the core. This topology can have different variations.
- In a **single core topology**, all hosts are connected to the edge tier and all storage is

connected to the core tier. Fig 2.16 depicts the core and edge switches in a single- core topology.

> A **dual-core topology** can be expanded to include more core switches. However, to maintain the topology, it is essential that new ISLs are created to connect each edge switch to the new core switch that is added. Fig 2.17 illustrates the core and edge switches in a dual-core topology.

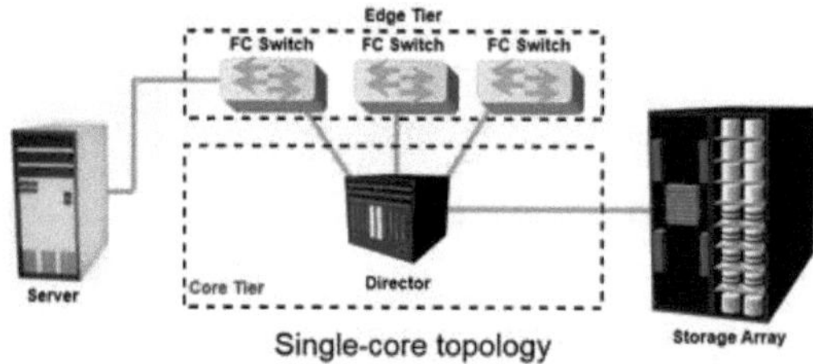

Fig 2.16: Single-core topology

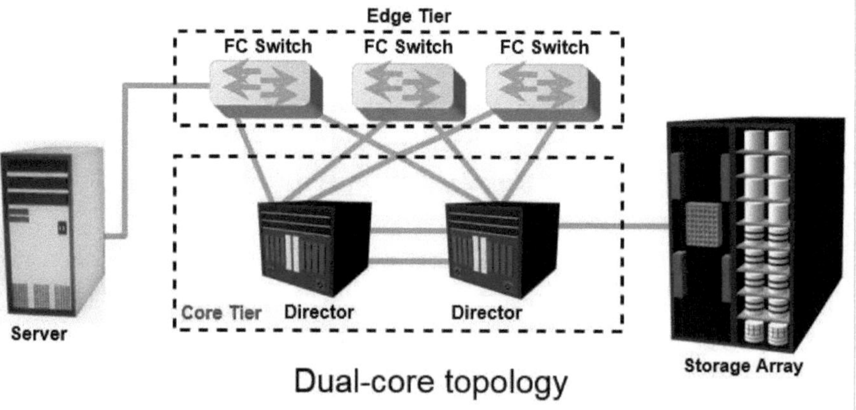

Fig 2.17: multi-core topology

Benefits and Limitations of Core-Edge Fabric

➢ The core-edge fabric provides one-hop storage access to all storage in the system. Because traffic travels in a deterministic pattern (from the edge to the core), a core-edge provides easier calculation of ISL loading and traffic patterns.

➢ Because each tier's switch is used for either storage or hosts, one can easily identify which resources are approaching their capacity, making it easier to develop a set of rules for scaling and apportioning.

➢ Core-edge fabrics can be scaled to larger environments by linking core switches, adding more core switches, or adding more edge switches.

➢ However, the core-edge fabric may lead to some performance-related problems because scaling a core-edge topology involves increasing the number of ISLs in the fabric.

➢ As more edge switches are added, the domain count in the fabric increases.

As the number of cores increases, it is prohibitive to continue to maintain ISLs from each core to each edge switch. When this happens, the fabric design is changed to a **compound or complex core-edge design.**

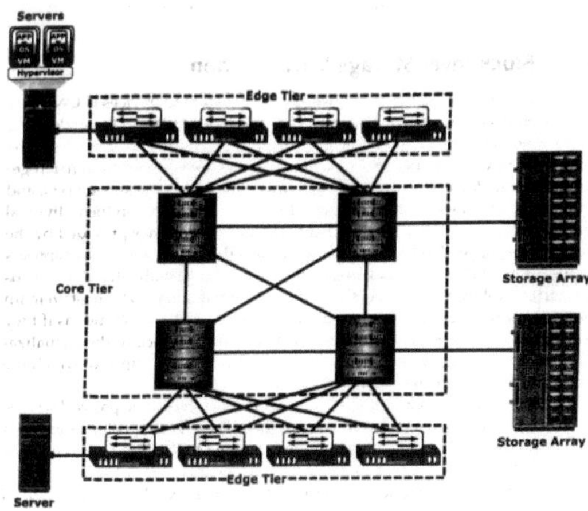

Fig 2.18: Compound core-edge topology

2.8 SAN based virtualization and VSAN technology

There are two network-based virtualization techniques in a SAN environment:
- block-level storage virtualization
- virtual SAN (VSAN).

Block-level Storage Virtualization

- *Block-level storage virtualization* aggregates block storage devices (LUNs) and enables provisioning of virtual storage volumes, independent of the underlying physical storage.

- A virtualization layer, which exists at the SAN, abstracts the identity of physical storage devices and creates a storage pool from heterogeneous storage devices.

- Virtual volumes are created from the storage pool and assigned to the hosts.

- Instead of being directed to the LUNs on the individual storage arrays, the hosts are directed to the virtual volumes provided by the virtualization layer.

- For hosts and storage arrays, the virtualization layer appears as the target and initiator devices, respectively.

- The virtualization layer maps the virtual volumes to the LUNs on the individual arrays.

- The hosts remain unaware of the mapping operation and access the virtual volumes as if they were accessing the physical storage attached to them.

- Typically, the virtualization layer is managed via a dedicated virtualization appliance to which the hosts and the storage arrays are connected.

- Fig 2.19 illustrates a virtualized environment. It shows two physical servers, each of which has one virtual volume assigned. These virtual volumes are used by the servers. These virtual volumes are mapped to the LUNs in the storage arrays.

- When an I/O is sent to a virtual volume, it is redirected through the virtualization layer at the storage network to the mapped LUNs.

- Depending on the capabilities of the virtualization appliance, the architecture may allow for more complex mapping between array LUNs and virtual volumes.

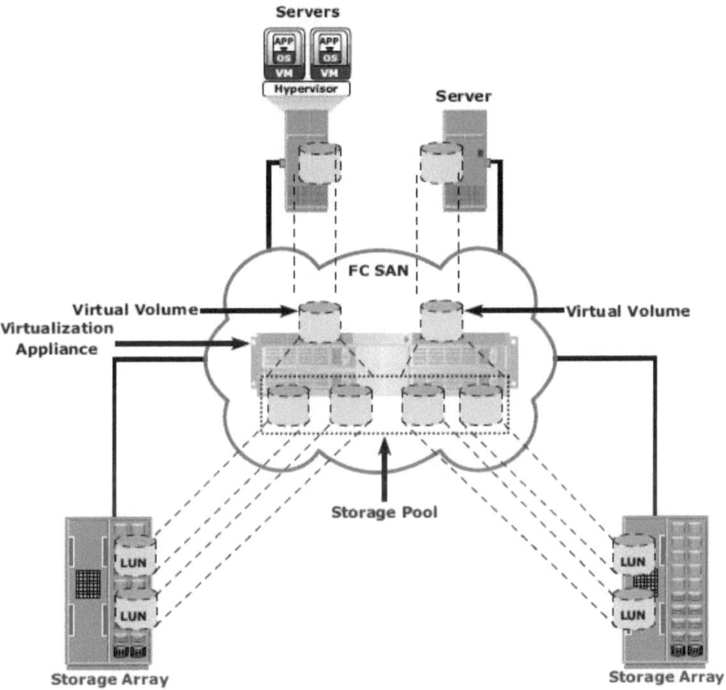

Fig 2.19 Block-level storage virtualization

- Block-level storage virtualization also provides the advantage of nondisruptive data migration.

- In a traditional SAN environment, LUN migration from one array to another is an offline event because the hosts needed to be updated to reflect the new array configuration.

- In other instances, host CPU cycles were required to migrate data from one array to the other, especially in a multivendor environment.

- With a block-level virtualization as a solution, the virtualization layer handles the back-end migration of data, which enables LUNs to remain online and accessible while data is migrating.

- No physical changes are required because the host still points to the same virtual targets on the virtualization layer.

- Previously, block-level storage virtualization provided nondisruptive data migration only within a data center. The new generation of block-level storage virtualization enables nondisruptive data migration both within and between data centers.

- It provides the capability to connect the virtualization layers at multiple data centers. The connected virtualization layers are managed centrally and work as a single virtualization layer stretched across data centers (Fig 2.20). This enables the federation of block-storage resources both within and across data centers. The virtual volumes are created from the federated storage resources.

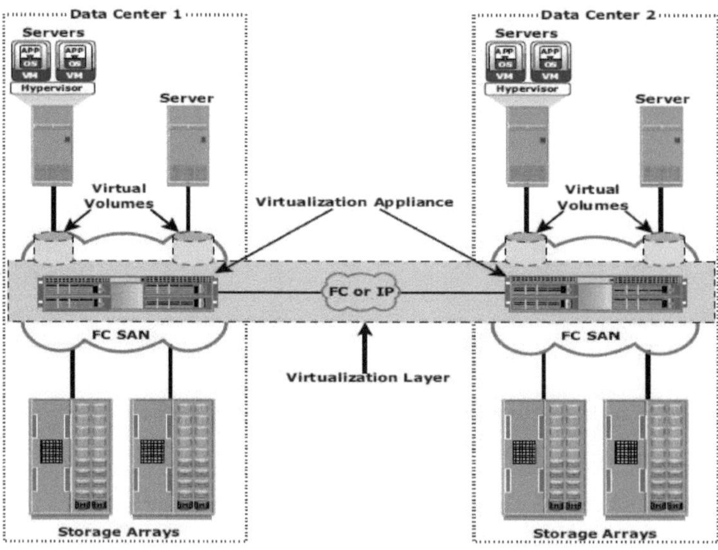

Fig 2.20 Federation of block storage across data centers

Virtual SAN (VSAN)

- *Virtual SAN* (also called *virtual fabric*) is a logical fabric on an FC SAN, which enables communication among a group of nodes regardless of their physical location in the fabric.

- In a VSAN, a group of hosts or storage ports communicate with each other using a virtual topology defined on the physical SAN.

- Multiple VSANs may be created on a single physical SAN.

- Each VSAN acts as an independent fabric with its own set of fabric services, such as name server, and zoning.

- Fabric-related configurations in one VSAN do not affect the traffic in another.

- VSANs improve SAN security, scalability, availability, and manageability.

- VSANs facilitate an easy, flexible, and less expensive way to manage networks.

- Configuring VSANs is easier and quicker compared to building separate physical FC SANs for various node groups.

- To regroup nodes, an administrator simply changes the VSAN configurations without moving nodes and recabling.

2.9 iSCSI

- iSCSI is an IP based protocol that establishes and manages connections between host and storage over IP, as shown in Fig 2.21.

- iSCSI encapsulates SCSI commands and data into an IP packet and transports them using TCP/IP.

- iSCSI is widely adopted for connecting servers to storage because it is relatively inexpensive and easy to implement, especially in environments in which an FC SAN does not exist.

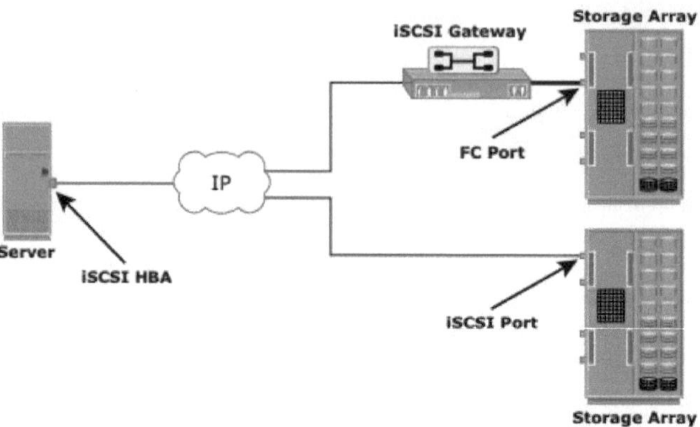

Fig 2.21: iSCSI implementation

2.9.1 Components of iSCSI

➤ An initiator (host), target (storage or iSCSI gateway), and an IP-based network are the key iSCSI components.

➤ If an iSCSI-capable storage array is deployed, then a host with the iSCSI initiator can directly communicate with the storage array over an IP network.

➤ However, in an implementation that uses an existing FC array for iSCSI communication, an iSCSI gateway is used.

➤ These devices perform the translation of IP packets to FC frames and vice versa, thereby bridging the connectivity between the IP and FC environments.

2.9.2 iSCSI Host Connectivity

The three iSCSI host connectivity options are:

- A standard NIC with software iSCSI initiator,

- a TCP offload engine (TOE) NIC with software iSCSI initiator,

- an iSCSI HBA

➢ The function of the iSCSI initiator is to route the SCSI commands over an IP network.

➢ A **standard NIC with a software iSCSI** initiator is the simplest and least expensive connectivity option. It is easy to implement because most servers come with at least one, and in many cases two, embedded NICs. It requires only a software initiator for iSCSI functionality. Because NICs provide standard IP function, encapsulation of SCSI into IP packets and decapsulation are carried out by the host CPU. This places additional overhead on the host CPU. If a standard NIC is used in heavy I/O load situations, the host CPU might become a bottleneck. TOE NIC helps reduce this burden.

➢ A **TOE NIC** offloads TCP management functions from the host and leaves only the iSCSI functionality to the host processor. The host passes the iSCSI information to the TOE card, and the TOE card sends the information to the destination using TCP/IP. Although this solution improves performance, the iSCSI functionality is still handled by a software initiator that requires host CPU cycles.

➢ An **iSCSI HBA** is capable of providing performance benefi ts because it offloads the entire iSCSI and TCP/IP processing from the host processor. The use of an iSCSI HBA is also the simplest way to boot hosts from a SAN environment via iSCSI. If there is no iSCSI HBA, modifi cations must be made to the basic operating system to boot a host from the storage devices because the NIC needs to obtain an IP address before the operating system loads. The functionality of an iSCSI HBA is similar to the functionality of an FC HBA.

2.9.3 iSCSI Topologies

➢ Two topologies of iSCSI implementations are **native and bridged**.

➢ Native topology does not have FC components.

➢ The initiators may be either directly attached to targets or connected through the IP network.

➢ Bridged topology enables the coexistence of FC with IP by providing iSCSI-to-FC bridging functionality.

➢ For example, the initiators can exist in an IP environment while the storage remains in an FC environment.

Native iSCSI Connectivity

> FC components are not required for iSCSI connectivity if an iSCSI-enabled array is deployed.

> In Fig 2.22(a), the array has one or more iSCSI ports configured with an IP address and is connected to a standard Ethernet switch.

> After an initiator is logged on to the network, it can access the available LUNs on the storage array.

> A single array port can service multiple hosts or initiators as long as the array port can handle the amount of storage traffic that the hosts generate.

Bridged iSCSI Connectivity

> A bridged iSCSI implementation includes FC components in its configuration.

> Fig 2.22(b), illustrates iSCSI host connectivity to an FC storage array. In this case, the array does not have any iSCSI ports. Therefore, an external device, called a gateway or a multiprotocol router, must be used to facilitate the communication between the iSCSI host and FC storage.

> The gateway converts IP packets to FC frames and vice versa.

> The bridge devices contain both FC and Ethernet ports to facilitate the communication between the FC and IP environments.

> In a bridged iSCSI implementation, the iSCSI initiator is configured with the gateway's IP address as its target destination.

> On the other side, the gateway is configured as an FC initiator to the storage array.

> **Combining FC and Native iSCSI Connectivity:** The most common topology is a

combination of FC and native iSCSI. Typically, a storage array comes with both FC and iSCSI ports that enable iSCSI and FC connectivity in the same environment, as shown in Fig 2.22(c).

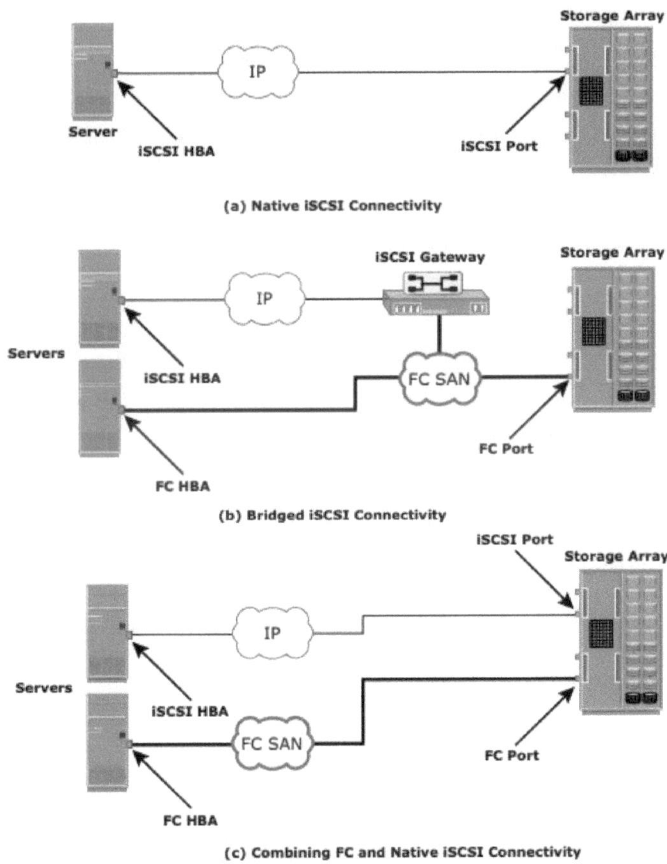

Fig 2.22 : iSCSI Topologies

➢ Fig 2.23 displays a model of the iSCSI protocol layers and depicts the encapsulation order of the SCSI commands for their delivery through a physical carrier.

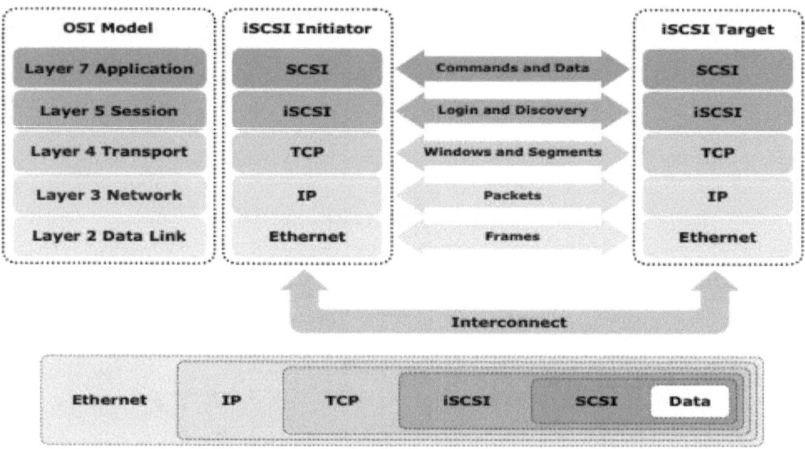

Fig 2.23: iSCSI protocol stack

➢ SCSI is the command protocol that works at the application layer of the Open System Interconnection (OSI) model.

➢ The initiators and targets use SCSI commands and responses to talk to each other.

➢ The SCSI command descriptor blocks, data, and status messages are encapsulated into TCP/IP and transmitted across the network between the initiators and targets.

➢ iSCSI is the session-layer protocol that initiates a reliable session between devices that recognize SCSI commands and TCP/IP.

➢ The iSCSI session-layer interface is responsible for handling login, authentication, target discovery, and session management.

➢ TCP is used with iSCSI at the transport layer to provide reliable transmission.

- ➢ TCP controls message flow, windowing, error recovery, and retransmission.

- ➢ It relies upon the network layer of the OSI model to provide global addressing and connectivity.

- ➢ The Layer 2 protocols at the data link layer of this model enable node-to-node communication through a physical network.

2.9.5 iSCSI PDU

- ➢ A *protocol data unit* (PDU) is the basic "information unit" in the iSCSI environment.

- ➢ The iSCSI initiators and targets communicate with each other using iSCSI PDUs. This communication includes establishing iSCSI connections and iSCSI sessions, performing iSCSI discovery, sending SCSI commands and data, and receiving SCSI status.

- ➢ All iSCSI PDUs contain one or more header segments followed by zero or more data segments.

- ➢ The PDU is then encapsulated into an IP packet to facilitate the transport.

- ➢ A PDU includes the components shown in Fig 2.23.

- ➢ The IP header provides packet-routing information to move the packet across a network.

- ➢ The TCP header contains the information required to guarantee the packet delivery to the target.

- ➢ The iSCSI header (basic header segment) describes how to extract SCSI commands and data for the target. iSCSI adds an optional CRC, known as the *digest*, to ensure datagram integrity. This is in addition to TCP checksum and Ethernet CRC.

- ➢ The header and the data digests are optionally used in the PDU to validate integrity and data placement.

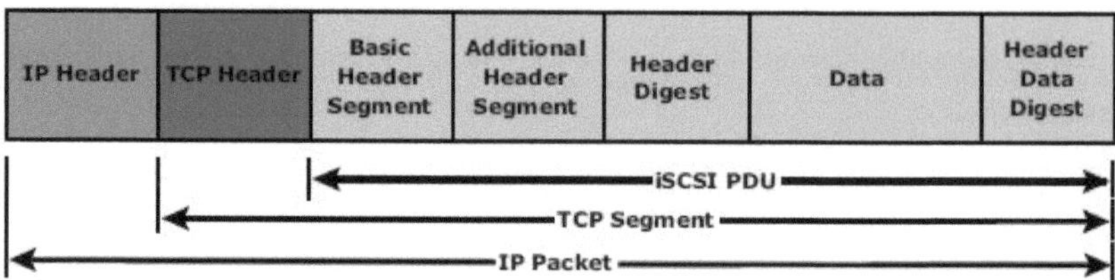

Fig 2.23 iSCSI PDU encapsulated in an IP packet

2.9.6 iSCSI Discovery

- An initiator must discover the location of its targets on the network and the names of the targets available to it before it can establish a session.

- This discovery can take place in two ways:

  - **SendTargets discovery**

  - **internet Storage Name Service (iSNS).**

- In *SendTargets discovery*, the initiator is manually configured with the target's network portal to establish a discovery session. The initiator issues the SendTargets command, and the target network portal responds with the names and addresses of the targets available to the host.

- iSNS (Fig 2.24) enables automatic discovery of iSCSI devices on an IP network. The initiators and targets can be configured to automatically register themselves with the iSNS server. Whenever an initiator wants to now the targets that it can access, it can query the iSNS server for a list of available targets.

- The discovery can also take place by using service location protocol (SLP). However, this is less commonly used than SendTargets discovery and iSNS.

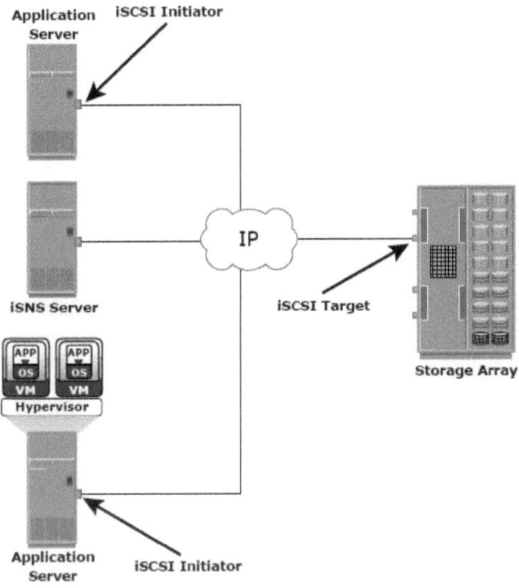

Fig 2.24 : Discovery using iSNS

2.9.7 iSCSI Names

> A unique worldwide iSCSI identifier, known as an *iSCSI name*, is used to identify the initiators and targets within an iSCSI network to facilitate communication.

> The unique identifier can be a combination of the names of the department, application, or manufacturer, serial number, asset number, or any tag that can be used to recognize and manage the devices.

> Following are two types of iSCSI names commonly used:

- **iSCSI Qualified Name (IQN):**
- **Extended Unique Identifier (EUI)**

➢ **iSCSI Qualified Name (IQN):** An organization must own a registered domain name to generate iSCSI Qualifi ed Names. This domain name does not need to be active or resolve to an address. It just needs to be reserved to prevent other organizations from using the same domain name to generate iSCSI names. A date is included in the name to avoid potential conflicts caused by the transfer of domain names.

An example of an IQN is iqn.2008-02.com.example:*optional_string*. The *optional_string* provides a serial number, an asset number, or any otherdevice identifiers.

➢ **Extended Unique Identifi er (EUI):** An EUI is a globally unique identifier based on the IEEE EUI-64 naming standard. An EUI is composed of the eui prefix followed by a 16-character hexadecimal name, such aseui.0300732A32598D26.

➢ In either format, the allowed special characters are dots, dashes, and blank spaces.

2.9.8 iSCSI Session

➢ An iSCSI session is established between an initiator and a target, as shown in Fig 2.25.

➢ A session is identified by a session ID (SSID), which includes part of an initiator ID and a target ID.

➢ The session can be intended for one of the following:

- The discovery of the available targets by the initiators and the location of a specific target on a network

- The normal operation of iSCSI (transferring data between initiators and targets)

➢ There might be one or more TCP connections within each session. Each TCP connection within the session has a unique connection ID (CID).

➢ An iSCSI session is established via the iSCSI login process. The login process is started when the initiator establishes a TCP connection with the required target either via the well-known port 3260 or a specified target port.

- During the login phase, the initiator and the target authenticate each other and negotiate on various parameters.

- After the login phase is successfully completed, the iSCSI session enters the full-feature phase for normal SCSI transactions. In this phase, the initiator may send SCSI commands and data to the various LUNs on the target.

- The final phase of the iSCSI session is the connection termination phase, which is referred to as the logout procedure.

- The initiator is responsible for commencing the logout procedure; however, the target may also prompt termination by sending an iSCSI message, indicating the occurrence of an internal error condition.

- After the logout request is sent from the initiator and accepted by the target, no further request and response can be sent on that connection.

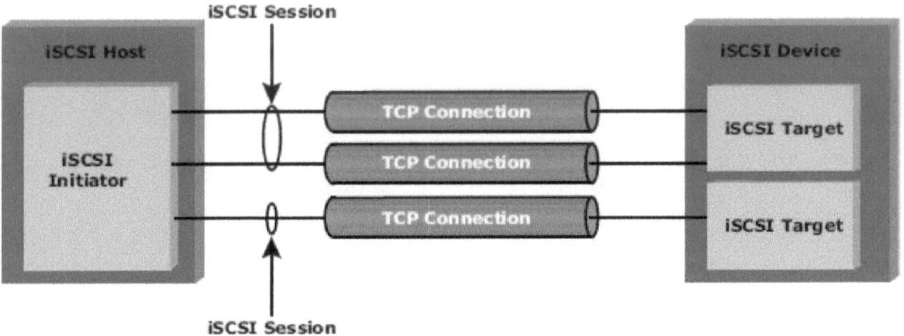

Fig 2.25 iSCSI session

2.9.9 Command Sequencing

- The iSCSI communication between the initiators and targets is based on the request-response command sequences.

- A command sequence may generate multiple PDUs.

➤ A *command sequence number* (**CmdSN**) within an iSCSI session is used for numbering all initiator-to-target command PDUs belonging to the session.

➤ This number ensures that every command is delivered in the same order in which it is transmitted, regardless of the TCP connection that carries the command in the session.

➤ Command sequencing begins with the first login command, and the CmdSN is incremented by one for each subsequent command.

➤ The iSCSI target layer is responsible for delivering the commands to the SCSI layer in the order of their CmdSN.

➤ Similar to command numbering, a *status sequence number* (**StatSN**) is used to sequentially number status responses, as shown in Fig 2.26.

➤ These unique numbers are established at the level of the TCP connection.

➤ A target sends *request-to-transfer* (**R2T**) PDUs to the initiator when it is ready to accept data.

➤ A *data sequence number* (DataSN) is used to ensure in-order delivery of data within the same command.

➤ The DataSN and R2TSN are used to sequence data PDUs and R2Ts, respectively.

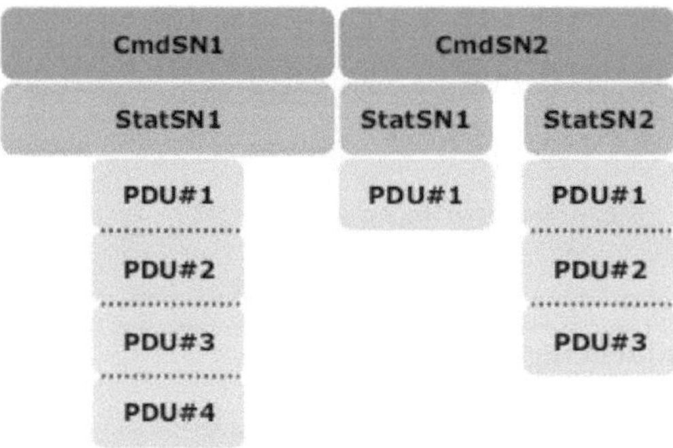

Fig 2.26 Command and status sequence number

2.10 FCIP (Fibre channel over IP)

> FCIP is a IP-based protocol that is used to connect distributed FC-SAN islands.

> Creates virtual FC links over existing IP network that is used to transport FC data between different FC SANS.

> It encapsulates FC frames into IP packet.

> It provides disaster recovery solution.

2.10.1 FCIP Protocol Stack

> The FCIP protocol stack is shown in Fig 2.27. Applications generate SCSI commands and data, which are processed by various layers of the protocol stack.

> The upper layer protocol SCSI includes the SCSI driver program that executes the read-and-write commands.

> Below the SCSI layer is the Fibre Channel Protocol (FCP) layer, which is simply a Fibre Channel frame whose payload is SCSI.

> The FCP layer rides on top of the Fibre Channel transport layer. This enables the FC frames to run natively within a SAN fabric environment. In addition, the FC frames can be encapsulated into the IP packet and sent to a remote SAN over the IP.

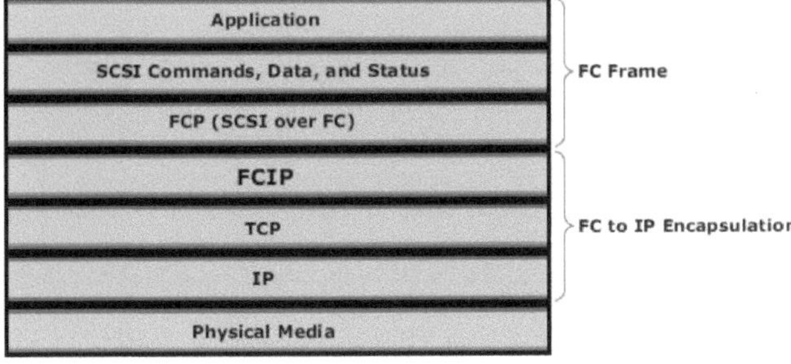

Fig 2.27 FCIP protocol stack

> The FCIP layer encapsulates the Fibre Channel frames onto the IP payload and passes them to the TCP layer (see Fig 2.28). TCP and IP are used for transporting the encapsulated information across Ethernet, wireless, or other media that support the TCP/IP traffic.

> Encapsulation of FC frame into an IP packet could cause the IP packet to be fragmented when the data link cannot support the maximum transmission unit (MTU) size of an IP packet.

> When an IP packet is fragmented, the required parts of the header must be copied by all fragments.

> When a TCP packet is segmented, normal TCP operations are responsible for receiving and re-sequencing the data prior to passing it on to the FC processing portion of the device.

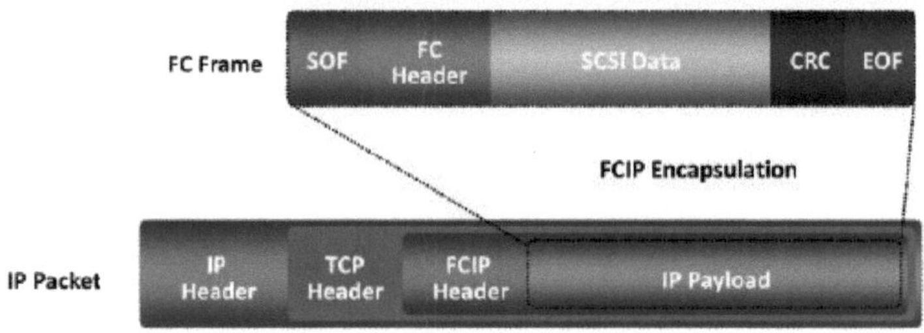

Fig 2.28 FCIP encapsulation

2.10.2 FCIP Topology

> In an FCIP environment, an FCIP gateway is connected to each fabric via a standard FC connection (Fig 2.29).

> The FCIP gateway at one end of the IP network encapsulates the FC frames into IP packets.

> The gateway at the other end removes the IP wrapper and sends the FC data to the layer 2 fabric.

> The fabric treats these gateways as layer 2 fabric switches.

> An IP address is assigned to the port on the gateway, which is connected to an IP network. After the IP connectivity is established, the nodes in the two independent fabrics can communicate

with each other.

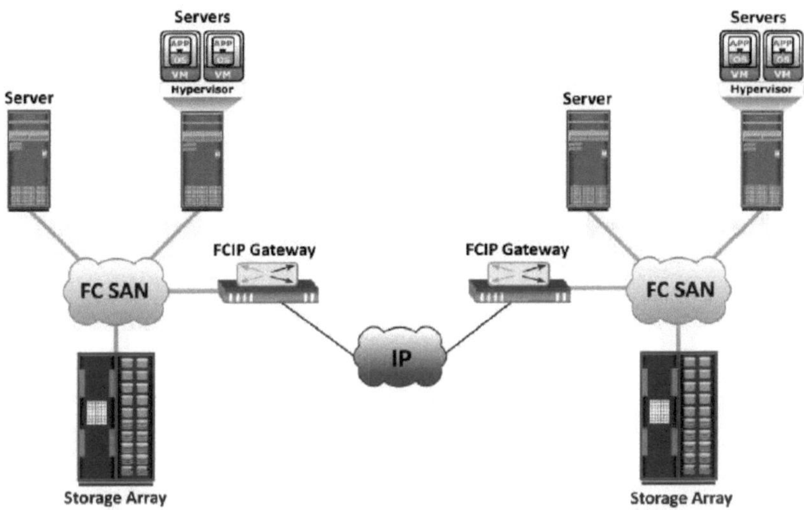

Fig 2.29 FCIP topology

2.11 FCoE (Fibre Channel over Ethernet)

➤ Data centers typically have multiple networks to handle various types of I/O traffic — for example, an Ethernet network for TCP/IP communication and an FC network for FC communication.

➤ TCP/IP is typically used for client-server communication, data backup, infrastructure management communication, and so on.

➤ FC is typically used for moving block-level data between storage and servers.

➤ To support multiple networks, servers in a data center are equipped with multiple redundant physical network interfaces — for example, multiple Ethernet and FC cards/adapters. In addition, to enable the communication, different types of networking switches and physical cabling infrastructure are implemented in data centers.

➢ The need for two different kinds of physical network infrastructure increases the overall cost and complexity of data center operation.

➢ Fibre Channel over Ethernet (FCoE) protocol provides consolidation of LAN and SAN traffic over a single physical interface infrastructure.

➢ FCoE helps organizations address the challenges of having multiple discrete network infrastructures.

➢ FCoE uses the Converged Enhanced Ethernet (CEE) link (10 Gigabit Ethernet) to send FC frames over Ethernet.

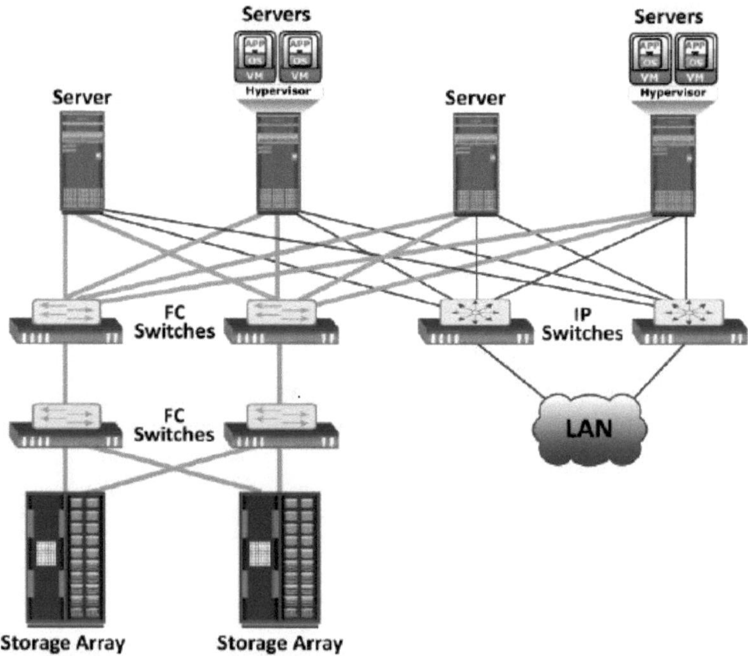

Fig 2.30 Before using FCOE

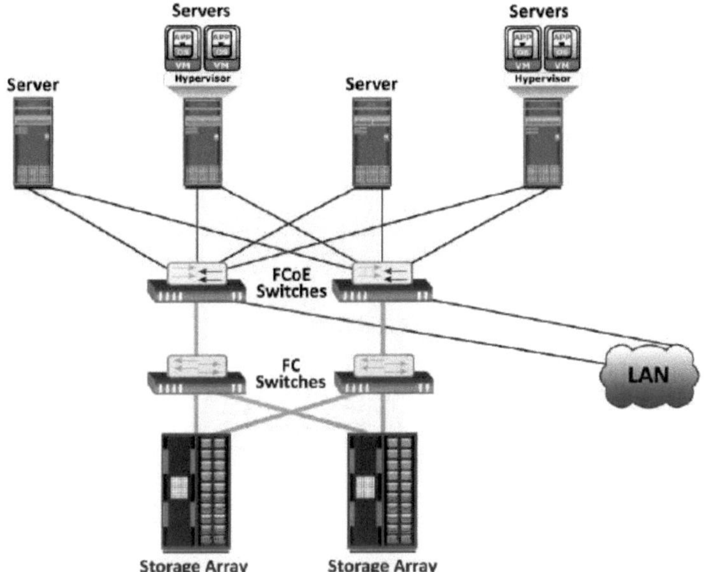

Fig 2.30 After using FCOE

2.11.1 Components of FCOE

The key components of FCOE are :

- ➢ Converged Network Adaptors(CNA)
- ➢ Cables
- ➢ FCOE Switches

Converged Network Adaptors(CNA)

➢ A CNA provides the functionality of both a standard NIC and an FC HBA in a single adapter and consolidates both types of traffic. CNA eliminates the need to deploy separate adapters and cables for FC and Ethernet communications, thereby reducing the required number of server slots and switch ports.

➢ As shown in Fig 2.31, a CNA contains separate modules for 10 Gigabit Ethernet, Fibre Channel, and FCoE Application Specific Integrated Circuits (ASICs). The FCoE ASIC encapsulates FC frames into Ethernet frames. One end of this ASIC is connected to 10GbE and FC ASICs for server connectivity, while the other end provides a 10GbE interface to connect to an FCoE switch.

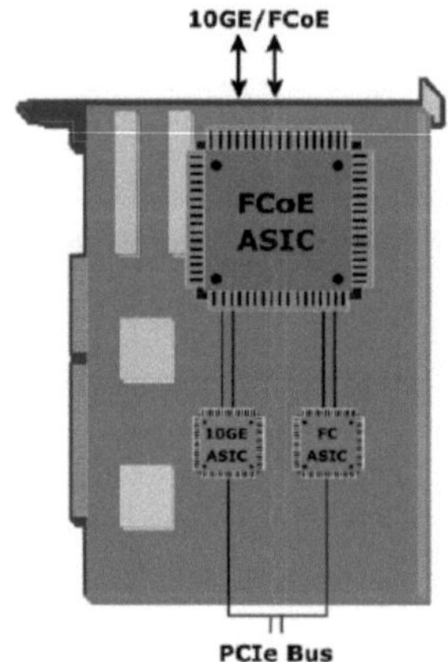

Fig 2.31 Converged Network Adapter

Cables

➢ There are two options available for FCoE cabling:

1. Copper based Twinax

2. standard fiber optical cables.

➢ A Twinax cable is composed of two pairs of copper cables covered with a shielded casing. The Twinax cable can transmit data at the speed of 10 Gbps over shorter distances up to 10 meters. Twinax cables require less power and are less expensive than fi ber optic cables.

➢ The Small Form Factor Pluggable Plus (SFP+) connector is the primary connector used for FCoE links and can be used with both optical and copper cables.

FCoE Switches

➤ An FCoE switch has both **Ethernet switch** and **Fibre Channel switch** functionalities.

➤ As shown in Fig 2.32, FCoE switch consists of:

   1. *Fibre Channel Forwarder (FCF)*,

   2. *Ethernet Bridge*,

   3. set of Ethernet ports

   4. optional FC ports

➤ The function of the FCF is to encapsulate the FC frames, received from the FC port, into the FCoE frames and also to de-encapsulate the FCoE frames, received from the Ethernet Bridge, to the FC frames.

➤ Upon receiving the incoming traffic, the FCoE switch inspects the **Ethertype** (used to indicate which protocol is encapsulated in the payload of an Ethernet frame) of the incoming frames and uses that to determine the destination.

   • If the Ethertype of the frame is FCoE, the switch recognizes that the frame contains an FC payload and forwards it to the FCF. From there, the FC is extracted from the FCoE frame and transmitted to FC SAN over the FC ports.

   • If the Ethertype is not FCoE, the switch handles the traffic as usual Ethernet traffic and forwards it over the Ethernet ports.

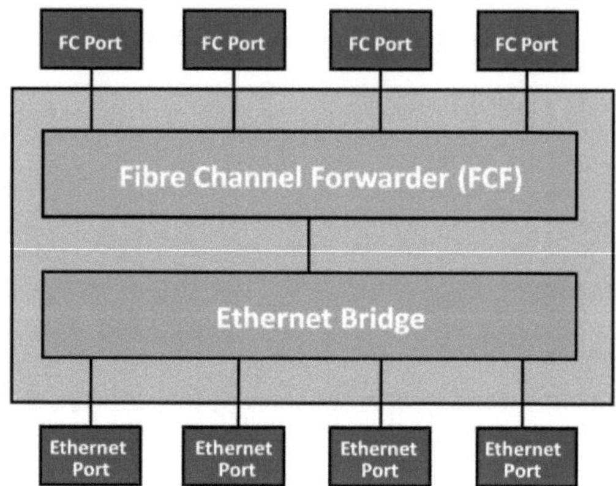

Fig 2.32 FCoE switch generic architecture

2.12 NETWORK ATTACHED STORAGE (NAS)

File Sharing Environment

➢ File sharing enables users to share files with other users

➢ In file-sharing environment, the creator or owner of a file determines the type of access to be given to other users and controls changes to the file.

➢ When multiple access a shared file at the same time, a locking scheme is required to maintain data integrity and also make this sharing possible. This is taken care by file-sharing environment.

➢ Examples of file sharing methods:

- File Transfer Protocol (FTP)

- Distributed File System (DFS)

- Network File System (NFS) and Common Internet File System (CIFS)

- Peer-to-Peer (P2P)

What is NAS?

➢ NAS is an IP based dedicated, high-performance file sharing and storage device.

➢ Enables NAS clients to share files over an IP network.

➢ Uses network and file-sharing protocols to provide access to the file data.

➢ Ex: Common Internet File System (CIFS) and Network File System (NFS).

➢ Enables both UNIX and Microsoft Windows users to share the same data seamlessly.

➢ NAS device uses its own operating system and integrated hardware and software components to meet specific file-service needs.

➢ Its operating system is optimized for file I/O which performs better than a general-purpose server.

➢ A NAS device can serve more clients than general-purpose servers and provide the benefit of server consolidation.

2.12.1 Components of NAS

➢ NAS device has *two* key components (as shown in Fig 2.33): **NAS head** and **storage**.

➢ In some NAS implementations, the storage could be external to the NAS device and shared with other hosts.

➢ NAS head includes the following components:

- CPU and memory

- One or more network interface cards (NICs), which provide connectivity to the client network.

- An optimized operating system for managing the NAS functionality. It translates file-level requests into block-storage requests and further converts the data supplied at the block level to file data

- NFS, CIFS, and other protocols for file sharing

- Industry-standard storage protocols and ports to connect and manage physical disk resources

➤ The NAS environment includes clients accessing a NAS device over an IP network using file-sharing protocols.

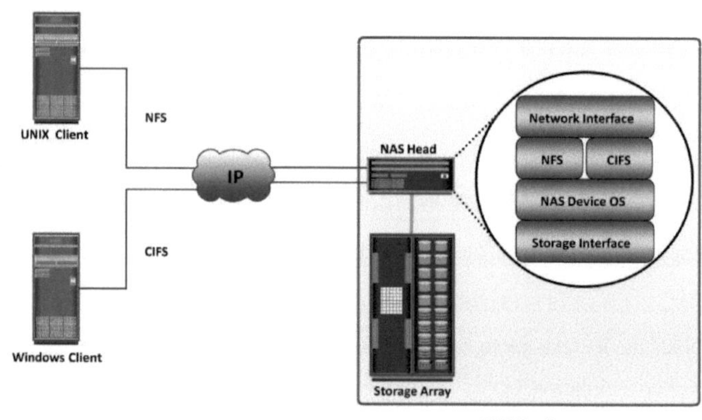

Fig 2.33 Components of NAS

2.12.2 NAS I/O Operation

➤ NAS provides *file-level data access* to its clients. File I/O is a high-level request that specifies the file to be accessed.

➤ Eg: a client may request a file by specifying its name, location, or other attributes. The NAS operating system keeps track of the location of files on the disk volume and converts client file I/O into block-level I/O to retrieve data.

➤ The process of handling I/Os in a NAS environment is as follows:

1. The requestor (client) packages an I/O request into TCP/IP and forwards it through the network stack. The NAS device receives this request from the network.

2. The NAS device converts the I/O request into an appropriate physical storage request,

which is a block-level I/O, and then performs the operation on the physical storage.

3. When the NAS device receives data from the storage, it processes and repackages the data into an appropriate file protocol response.

4. The NAS device packages this response into TCP/IP again and forwards it to the client through the network.

➢ Fig 2.34 illustrates the NAS I/O operation

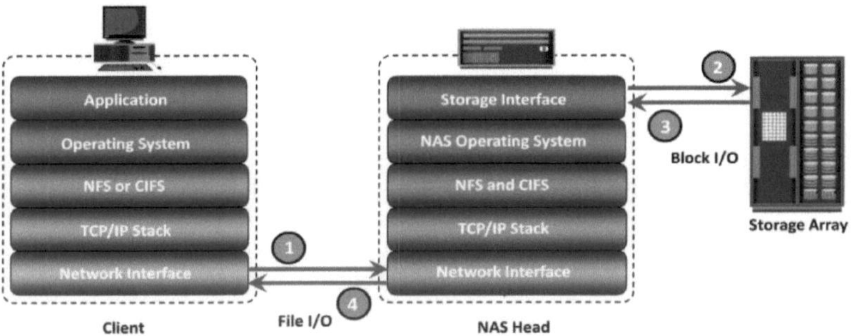

Fig 2.34 NAS I/O Operation

2.12.3 NAS File Sharing Protocols

➢ NAS devices support multiple file-service protocols to handle file I/O requests

➢ Two common NAS file sharing protocols are:

- Common Internet File System (CIFS)

- Network File System (NFS)

➢ NAS devices enable users to share file data across different operating environments

➢ It provides a means for users to migrate transparently from one operating system to another

Network File System (NFS)

➢ NFS is a **client-server protocol** for file sharing that is commonly used on **UNIX systems**.

➢ NFS was originally based on the connectionless *User Datagram Protocol (UDP)*.

➢ It uses *Remote Procedure Call (RPC)* as a method of inter-process communication between two computers.

➢ The NFS protocol provides a set of RPCs to access a remote file system for the following operations:

- Searching files and directories
- Opening, reading, writing to, and closing a file
- Changing file attributes
- Modifying file links and directories

➢ NFS creates a connection between the client and the remote system to transfer data.

➢ NFSv3 and earlier is a stateless protocol

➢ It does not maintain any kind of table to store information about open files and associated pointers. Each call provides a full set of arguments - a file handle, a particular position to read or write, and the versions of NFS - to access files on the server .

➢ Currently, three versions of NFS are in use:
1. **NFS version 2 (NFSv2):** Uses *UDP* to provide a *stateless* network connection between a client and a server. Features, such as locking, are handled outside the protocol.
2. **NFS version 3 (NFSv3):** Uses *UDP or TCP*, and is based on the *stateless protocol* design. It includes some new features, such as a 64-bit file size, asynchronous writes, and additional file attributes to reduce refetching.
3. **NFS version 4 (NFSv4):** Uses TCP and is based on a *stateful protocol* design. It offers enhanced security. The latest NFS version 4.1 is the enhancement of NFSv4 and includes some new features, such as session model, parallel NFS (pNFS), and data retention.

Common Internet File System (CIFS)

➢ CIFS is a *client-server application* protocol

➢ It enables clients to access files and services on remote computers over **TCP/IP**.

➢ It is a public, or open, variation of **Server Message Block (SMB)** protocol.

➢ It provides following features to ensure data integrity:

- It uses file and record locking to prevent users from overwriting the work of another user on a file or a record.

- It supports fault tolerance and can automatically restore connections and reopen files that were open prior to an interruption. This feature depends on whether an application is written to take advantage of this.

- CIFS is a stateful protocol because the CIFS server maintains connection information regarding every connected client. If a network failure or CIFS server failure occurs, the client receives a disconnection notification. User disruption is minimized if the application has the embedded intelligence to restore the connection. However, if the embedded intelligence is missing, the user must take steps to reestablish the CIFS connection.

➢ Users refer to remote file systems with an easy-to-use file-naming scheme:

➢ Eg: \\server\share or \\servername.domain.suffix\share

2.13 File-level Virtualization

➢ File-level virtualization, implemented in NAS or the file server environment, provides a simple, non disruptive file-mobility solution.

➢ It eliminates the dependencies between data accessed at the file level and the location where the files are physically stored.

➢ It creates a logical pool of storage, enabling users to use a logical path, rather than a physical path, to access files.

➢ A global namespace is used to map the logical path of a file to the physical path names. File-level virtualization enables the movement of files across NAS devices, even if the files are being accessed.

Before and After File-level Virtualization

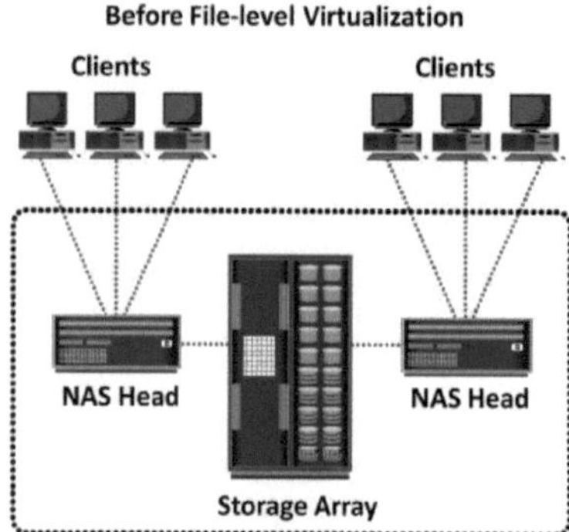

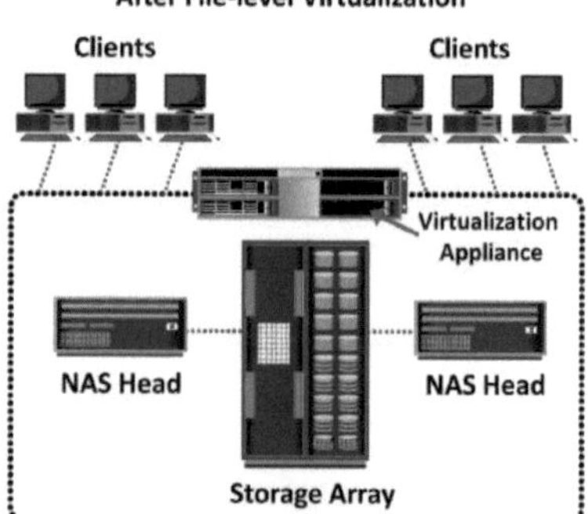

- Dependency between client access and file location
- Underutilized storage resources
- Downtime is caused by data migrations

- Break dependencies between client access and file location
- Storage utilization is optimized
- Non-disruptive migrations

Object-Based Storage & Unified Storage Platform

➤ **Object-based storage** is a way to store file data in the form of objects based on its *content and other attributes* rather than the name and location.

➤ Recent studies have shown that more than 90 percent of data generated is unstructured.

➤ Traditional NAS, which is the dominant solution for storing unstructured data, has become inefficient.

➤ This demands a smarter approach to manage unstructured data based on its content rather than metadata about its name, location, and so on.

➢ Due to varied application requirements, organizations have been deploying storage area networks (SANs), NAS, and object-based storage devices (OSDs) in their data centers.

➢ Deploying these disparate storage solutions adds management complexity, cost and environmental overhead.

➢ An ideal solution is to have an integrated storage solution that supports block, file, and object access.

➢ **Unified storage** has emerged as a solution that consolidates *block, file,* and *object-based access* within one unified platform.

➢ It supports multiple protocols for data access and can be managed using a single management interface.

2.14 Object-Based Storage Devices (OSD)

➢ An OSD is a device that *organizes and stores* unstructured data, such as movies, office documents, and graphics, as objects.

➢ **Object-based storage** provides a scalable, self-managed, protected, and shared storage option. OSD stores data in the form of objects.

➢ OSD uses *flat address space* to store data. Therefore, there is no hierarchy of directories and files; as a result, a large number of objects can be stored in an OSD system (see Fig 2.35).

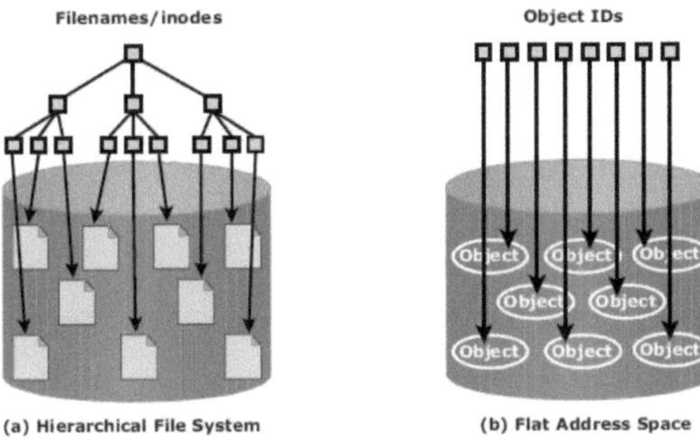

Fig 2.35 Hierarchical file system versus flat address space

➢ An object might contain user data, related metadata (size, date, ownership, and so on), and other attributes of data (retention, access pattern, and so on); See Fig 2.36.

➢ Each object stored in the system is identified by a unique ID called the **object ID**.

➢ The object ID is generated using specialized algorithms such as hash function on the data and guarantees that every object is uniquely identified.

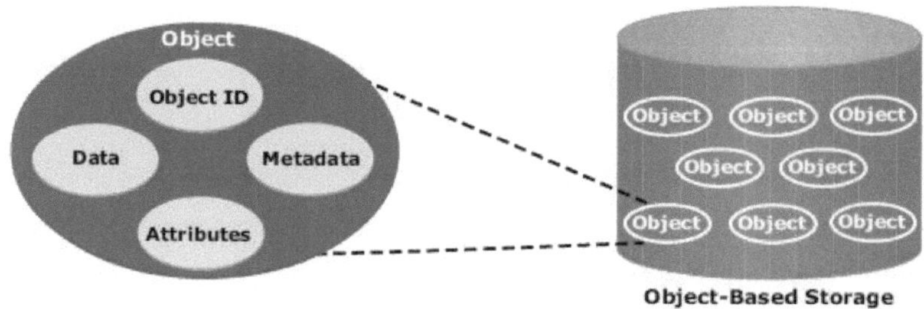

Fig 2.36 Object Structure

2.14.1 Object-Based Storage Architecture

➢ An I/O in the traditional block access method passes through various layers in the I/O path.

➢ The I/O generated by an application passes through the file system, the channel, or network and reaches the disk drive.

➢ When the file system receives the I/O from an application, the file system maps the incoming I/O to the disk blocks. The block interface is used for sending the I/O over the channel or network to the storage device. The I/O is then written to the block allocated on the disk drive.

➢ Fig 2.37 (a) illustrates the block-level access.

➢ The file system has two components: *user component* and *storage component.*

    1. The user component of the file system performs functions such as hierarchy management, naming, and user access control.

    2. The storage component maps the files to the physical location on the disk drive.

➢ When an application accesses data stored in OSD, the request is sent to the file system user component. The file system user component communicates to the OSD interface, which in turn sends the request to the storage device.

➢ The storage device has the OSD storage component responsible for managing the access to the object on a storage device.

➢ Fig 2.37 (b) illustrates the object-level access.

➢ After the object is stored, the OSD sends an acknowledgment to the application server.

➢ The OSD storage component manages all the required low-level storage and space management functions. It also manages security and access control functions for the objects.

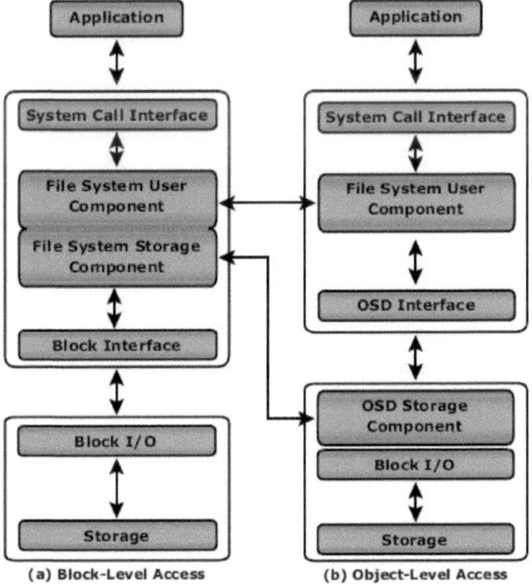

Fig 2.37 Block-level access versus object-level access

2.14.2 Components of OSD

➤ The OSD system is typically composed of three key components:

   1. nodes

   2. private network

   3. storage

➤ Fig 2.38 illustrates the components of OSD.

➤ A **node** is a server that runs the *OSD operating environment* and provides *services* to store, retrieve, and manage data in the system. The OSD system is composed of one or more nodes.

➤ The OSD node has *two* key services:

   1. The ***metadata service*** is responsible for generating the object ID from the contents of a file. It also maintains the mapping of the object IDs and the file system namespace.

   2. The ***storage service*** manages a set of disks on which the user data is stored.

➤ The OSD nodes connect to the storage via an **internal network (private network)**. The internal network provides node-to-node connectivity and node-to-storage connectivity.

➤ The application server accesses the node to store and retrieve data over an *external network*.

➤ For **storage,** OSD typically uses low-cost and high-density disk drives to store the objects. As more capacity is required, more disk drives can be added to the system.

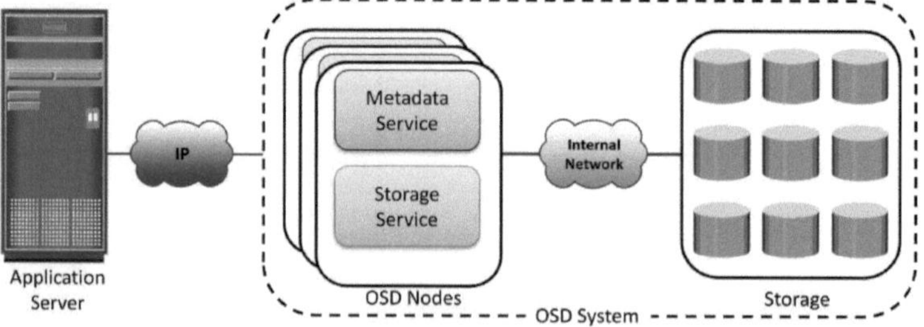

Fig 2.38: OSD Components

2.14.3 Object Storage and Retrieval in OSD

➢ The process of storing objects in OSD is illustrated in Fig 2.39.

➢ The data storage process in an OSD system is as follows:

1. The application server presents the file to be stored to the OSD node.

2. The OSD node divides the file into two parts: **user data** and **metadata**.

3. The OSD node generates the **object ID** using a specialized algorithm. The algorithm is executed against the contents of the user data to derive an ID unique to this data.

4. For future access, the OSD node stores the metadata and object ID using the *metadata service*.

5. The OSD node stores the user data (objects) in the storage device using the *storage service*.

6. An acknowledgment is sent to the application server stating that the object is stored.

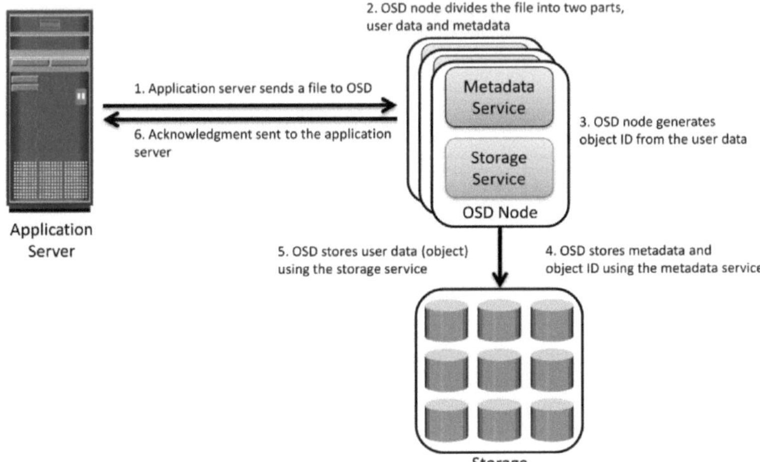

Fig 2.39: Storing objects on OSD

➤ The application server retrieves the stored content using the **object ID**. This process is transparent to the user.

➤ The process of retrieving objects in OSD is illustrated in Fig 2.40. The process of data retrieval from OSD is as follows:

1. The application server sends a ***read request*** to the OSD system.

2. The metadata service retrieves the object ID for the requested file.

3. The metadata service sends the object ID to the application server.

4. The application server sends the object ID to the OSD storage service for object retrieval.

5. The OSD storage service retrieves the object from the storage device.

6. The OSD storage service sends the file to the application server.

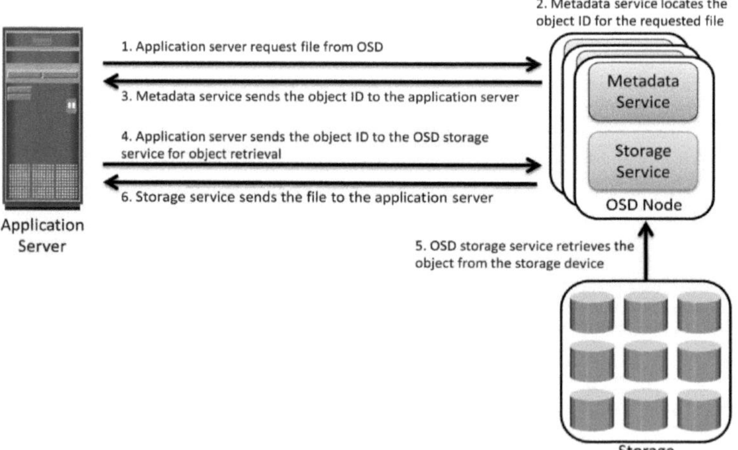

Fig 2.40: Object retrieval from an OSD system

2.14.4 Benefits of Object-Based Storage

➢ The key benefits of object-based storage are as follows:

- **Security and reliability:** Data integrity and content authenticity are the key features of object-based storage devices. OSD uses *specialized algorithms* to create objects that provide strong data encryption capability. In OSD, request authentication is performed at the storage device rather than with an external authentication mechanism.

- **Platform independence:** Objects are abstract containers of data, including metadata and attributes. This feature allows objects to be shared across heterogeneous platforms locally or remotely. This makes object-based storage the best candidate for cloud computing environments.

- **Scalability:** Due to the use of flat address space, object-based storage can handle large amounts of data without impacting performance. Both storage and OSD nodes can be scaled independently in terms of performance and capacity.

- **Manageability:** Object-based storage has an inherent intelligence to manage and protect objects. It uses self-healing capability to protect and replicate objects. Policy-based management capability helps OSD to handle routine jobs automatically.

2.14.5 Common Use Cases for Object-Based Storage

➢ A **data archival solution** is a promising use case for OSD. Data integrity and protection is the primary requirement for any data archiving solution. Traditional archival solutions - CD and DVD-ROM - do not provide scalability and performance. OSD stores data in the form of objects, associates them with a unique object ID, and ensures high data integrity. Along with integrity, it provides scalability and data protection. These capabilities make OSD a viable option for long term data archiving for fixed content.

➢ Cloud-based storage is another use case of OSD. OSD uses a web interface to access storage resources. OSD provides inherent security, scalability, and automated data management. It also enables data sharing across heterogeneous platforms or tenants while ensuring integrity of data.

These capabilities make OSD a strong option for cloud-based storage. Cloud service providers can leverage OSD to offer storage-as-a-service.

➢ OSD supports web service access via **representational state transfer (REST)** and **simple object access protocol (SOAP)**.

➢ REST and SOAP APIs can be easily integrated with business applications that access OSD over the web.

2.15 Unified Storage

➢ Unified storage consolidates *block, file,* and *object* access into one storage solution.

➢ It supports multiple protocols, such as CIFS, NFS, iSCSI, FC, FCoE, REST (representational state transfer), and SOAP (simple object access protocol).

2.15.1 Components of Unified Storage

➢ A unified storage system consists of the following key components:

- storage controller,

- NAS head,

- OSD node,

- storage.

➢ Fig 2.41 illustrates the block diagram of a unified storage platform.

➢ The **storage controller or storage processor** provides block-level access to application servers through iSCSI, FC, or FCoE protocols. It contains the corresponding front-end ports for direct block access. The storage controller is also responsible for managing the back-end storage pool in the storage system.

➢ The controller configures LUNs and presents them to application servers, NAS heads, and OSD nodes. The LUNs presented to the application server appear as local physical disks. A file system is configured on these LUNs and is made available to applications for storing data.

➢ **A NAS head** is a dedicated file server that provides file access to NAS clients. The NAS head is connected to the storage via the storage controller typically using a FC or FCoE connection. The system typically has two or more NAS heads for redundancy.

➢ The **LUNs** presented to the NAS head appear as physical disks. The NAS head configures the file systems on these disks, creates a NFS, CIFS, or mixed share, and exports the share to the NAS clients.

➢ **The OSD node** also accesses the storage through the storage controller using a FC or FCoE connection.

➢ The LUNs assigned to the OSD node appear as physical disks. These disks are configured by the OSD nodes, enabling them to store the data from the web application servers.

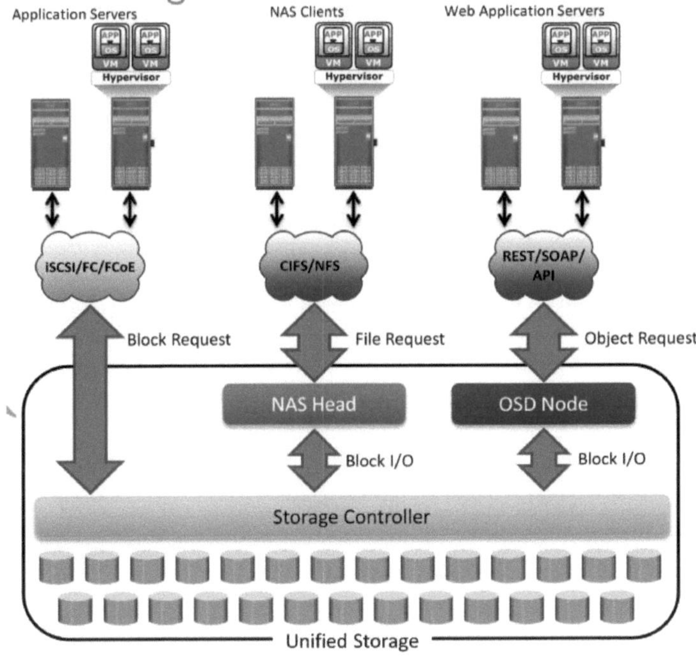

Fig 2.41 Unified Storage Platform

Data Access from Unified Storage

> In a unified storage system, block, file, and object requests to the storage travel through different I/O paths. Fig 2.41 also illustrates the different I/O paths for block, file, and object access.

> **Block I/O request:** The application servers are connected to an FC, iSCSI, or FCoE port on the storage controller. The server sends a block request and the storage processor (SP) processes the I/O and responds to the application server.

> **File I/O request:** The NAS clients send a file request to the NAS head using NFS or CIFS protocol. The NAS head receives the request, converts it into a block request, and forwards it to the storage controller. Upon receiving the block data, the NAS head again converts the block request back to the file request and sends back it to the clients.

> **Object I/O request:** The web application servers send an object request, typically using REST or SOAP protocols, to the OSD node. The OSD node receives the request, converts it into a block request, and sends it to the disk through the storage controller. The controller in turn processes the block request and responds back to the OSD node, which in turn provides the requested object to the web application server.

UNIT-III

BACKUP, ARCHIVE, AND REPLICATION

3.1 INTRODUCTION TO BUSINESS CONTINUITY

Business Continuity (BC):

Business continuity (BC) is an integrated and enterprise wide process that includes all activities (internal and external to IT) that a business must perform to mitigate the impact of planned and unplanned downtime.

BC entails preparing for, responding to, and recovering from a system outage that adversely affects business operations. It involves proactive measures, such as business impact analysis, risk assessments, deployment of BC technology solutions (backup and replication), and reactive measures, such as disaster recovery and restart, to be invoked in the event of a failure.

The goal of a BC solution is to ensure the **"information availability"** required to conduct vital business operations.

3.1.1 Information Availability:

Information availability (IA) refers to the ability of the infrastructure to function according to business expectations during its specified time of operation. Information availability ensures that people (employees, customers, suppliers, and partners) can access information whenever they need it. Information availability can be defined in terms of:

1. Reliability,
2. Accessibility
3. Timeliness.

1. **Reliability:** This reflects a component's ability to function without failure, under stated conditions, for a specified amount of time.
2. **Accessibility:** This is the state within which the required information is accessible at the right place, to the right user. The period of time during which the system is in an accessible state is termed **system uptime;** when it is not accessible it is termed **system**

downtime.

3. **Timeliness:** Defines the exact moment or the time window (a particular time of the day, week, month, and/or year as specified) during which information must be accessible. For example, if online access to an application is required between 8:00 am and 10:00 pm each day, any disruptions to data availability outside of this time slot are not considered to affect timeliness.

3.1.1.1   Causes of Information Unavailability

Various planned and unplanned incidents result in data unavailability.

➤ **Planned outages** include installation/integration/maintenance of new hardware, software upgrades or patches, taking backups, application and data restores, facility operations (renovation and construction), and refresh/migration of the testing to the production environment.

➤ **Unplanned outages** include failure caused by database corruption, component failure, and human errors.

➤ **Disasters (natural or man-made)** such as flood, fire, earthquake, and contamination are another type of incident that may cause data unavailability.

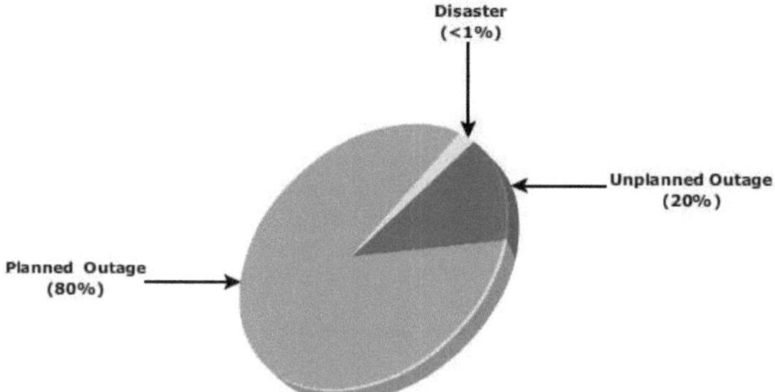

Fig 3.1: Disruptors of Information Availability

As illustrated in Fig 3.1 above, the majority of outages are planned. Planned outages are expected and scheduled, but still cause data to be unavailable.

3.1.1.2   Consequences of Downtime

➢ Information unavailability or downtime results in loss of productivity, loss of revenue, poor financial performance, and damage to reputation.

➢ Loss of productivity includes reduced output per unit of labor, equipment, and capital.

➢ Loss of revenue includes direct loss, compensatory payments, future revenue loss, billing loss, and investment loss.

➢ Poor financial performance affects revenue recognition, cash flow, discounts, payment guarantees, credit rating, and stock price.

➢ Damages to reputations may result in a loss of confidence or credibility with customers, suppliers, financial markets, banks, and business partners.

➢ An important metric, *average cost of downtime per hour*, provides a key estimate in determining the appropriate BC solutions. It is calculated as follows:

$$\text{Average cost of downtime per hour} = \text{average productivity loss per hour} +$$
$$\text{average revenue loss per hour}$$

Where:

$$\text{Productivity loss per hour} = \text{(total salaries and benefits of all employees per week)}$$
$$/\text{(average number of working hours per week)}$$
$$\text{Average revenue loss per hour} = \text{(total revenue of an organization per week)}$$
$$/\text{(average number of hours per week that an organization is open for business)}$$

3.1.1.3   Measuring Information Availability

➢ Information availability (IA) relies on the availability of physical and virtual components of a data center. Failure of these components might disrupt IA. A failure is the termination of a component's capability to perform a required function. The component's capability can be restored by performing an external corrective action, such as a manual reboot, a repair, or replacement of the failed component(s).

➢ Proactive risk analysis performed as part of the BC planning process considers the component failure rate and average repair time, which are measured by MTBF and MTTR:

→ **Mean Time Between Failure (MTBF):** It is the average time available for a system or component to perform its normal operations between failures.

→ **Mean Time To Repair (MTTR):** It is the average time required to repair a failed component. MTTR includes the total time required to do the following activities: Detect the fault, mobilize the maintenance team, diagnose the fault, obtain the spare parts, repair, test, and restore the data.

Fig 3.2 illustrates the various information availability metrics that represent system uptime and downtime.

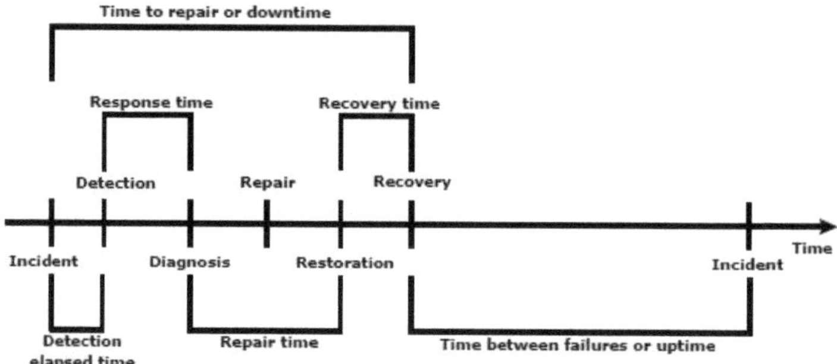

Fig 3-2: Information availability metrics

IA is the time period that a system is in a condition to perform its intended function upon demand. It can be expressed in terms of system uptime and downtime and measured as the amount or percentage of system uptime:

IA = system uptime / (system uptime + system downtime)

In terms of MTBF and MTTR, IA could also be expressed as

IA = MTBF / (MTBF + MTTR)

Uptime per year is based on the exact timeliness requirements of the service, this calculation leads to the number of "9s" representation for availability metrics.

Table 3-1 lists the approximate amount of downtime allowed for a service to achieve certain levels of 9s availability. For example, a service that is said to be "five 9s available" is available for 99.999 percent of the scheduled time in a year (24 × 365).

UPTIME (%)	DOWNTIME (%)	DOWNTIME PER YEAR	DOWNTIME PER WEEK
98	2	. 7.3 days	3 hr, 22 minutes
99	1	3.65 days	1 hr, 41 minutes
99.8	0.2	17 hr, 31 minutes	20 minutes, 10 secs
99.9	0.1	8 hr, 45 minutes	10 minutes, 5 secs
99.99	0.01	52.5 minutes	1 minute
99.999	0.001	5.25 minutes	6 secs
99.9999	0.0001	31.5 secs	0.6 secs

Table 3-1: Availability percentage and Allowable downtime

3.1.2 BC Terminology

This section defines common terms related to BC operations which are used in this module to explain advanced concepts:

➢ **Disaster recovery:** This is the coordinated process of restoring systems, data, and the infrastructure required to support key ongoing business operations in the event of a disaster. It is the process of restoring a previous copy of the data and applying logs or other necessary processes to that copy to bring it to a known point of consistency. Once all recoveries are completed, the data is validated to ensure that it is correct.

➢ **Disaster restart:** This is the process of restarting business operations with mirrored consistent copies of data and applications.

➢ **Recovery-Point Objective (RPO):** This is the point in time to which systems and data must be recovered after an outage. It defines the amount of data loss that a business can endure. A large RPO signifies high tolerance to information loss in a business. Based on the RPO, organizations plan for the minimum frequency with which a backup or replica must be made. For example, if the RPO is six hours, backups or replicas must be made at least once in 6 hours. Fig 3.3 (a) shows various RPOs and their corresponding ideal recovery strategies. An organization can plan for an appropriate BC technology solution on the basis of the RPO it sets. For example:

→ **RPO of 24 hours:** This ensures that backups are created on an offsite tape drive every midnight. The corresponding recovery strategy is to restore data from the set of last backup tapes.

→ **RPO of 1 hour:** Shipping database logs to the remote site every hour. The corresponding recovery strategy is to recover the database at the point of the last log shipment.

→ **RPO in the order of minutes:** Mirroring data asynchronously to a remote site

→ **Near zero RPO:** This mirrors mission-critical data synchronously to a remote site.

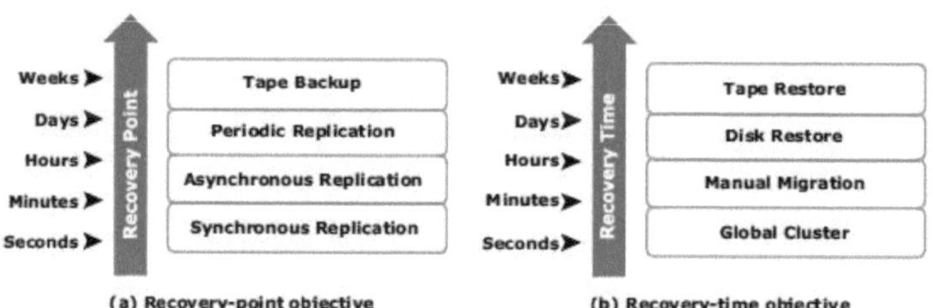

Fig 3.3: Strategies to meet RPO and RTO targets

➢ **Recovery-Time Objective (RTO):** The time within which systems and applications must be recovered after an outage. It defines the amount of downtime that a business can endure and survive. Businesses can optimize disaster recovery plans after defining the RTO for a given system. For example, if the RTO is two hours, then use a disk backup because it enables a faster restore than a tape backup. However, for an RTO of one week, tape backup will likely meet requirements. Some examples of RTOs and the recovery strategies to ensure data availability are listed below (refer to Fig 3.3 (b)):

→ **RTO of 72 hours:** Restore from backup tapes at a cold site.

→ **RTO of 12 hours:** Restore from tapes at a hot site.

→ **RTO of few hours:** Use a data vault to a hot site.

→ **RTO of a few seconds:** Cluster production servers with bidirectional mirroring, enabling the applications to run at both sites simultaneously.

3.1.3 BC Planning Life Cycle

BC planning must follow a disciplined approach like any other planning process. Organizations today dedicate specialized resources to develop and maintain BC plans. From the conceptualization to the realization of the BC plan, a life cycle of activities can be defined for the BC process.

The BC planning lifecycle includes five stages shown below (Fig 3.4):

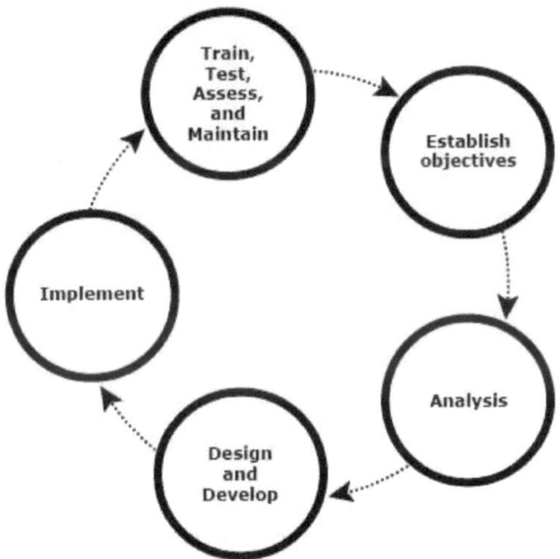

Fig 3.4: BC Planning Lifecycle

Several activities are performed at each stage of the BC planning lifecycle, including the following key activities:

1. **Establishing objectives**

→ Determine BC requirements.

→ Estimate the scope and budget to achieve requirements.

→ Select a BC team by considering subject matter experts from all areas of the business, whether internal or external.

→ Create BC policies.

2. Analyzing

→ Collect information on data profiles, business processes, infrastructure support, dependencies, and frequency of using business infrastructure.

→ Identify critical business needs and assign recovery priorities.

→ Create a risk analysis for critical areas and mitigation strategies.

→ Conduct a Business Impact Analysis (BIA).

→ Create a cost and benefit analysis based on the consequences of data unavailability.

3. Designing and developing

→ Define the team structure and assign individual roles and responsibilities. For example, different teams are formed for activities such as emergency response, damage assessment, and infrastructure and application recovery.

→ Design data protection strategies and develop infrastructure.

→ Develop contingency scenarios.

→ Develop emergency response procedures.

→ Detail recovery and restart procedures.

4. Implementing

→ Implement risk management and mitigation procedures that include backup, replication, and management of resources.

→ Prepare the disaster recovery sites that can be utilized if a disaster affects the primary data center.

→ Implement redundancy for every resource in a data center to avoid single points of failure.

5. Training, testing, assessing, and maintaining

→ Train the employees who are responsible for backup and replication of business-critical data on a regular basis or whenever there is a modification in the BC plan

→ Train employees on emergency response procedures when disasters are declared.

→ Train the recovery team on recovery procedures based on contingency scenarios.

→ Perform damage assessment processes and review recovery plans.

→ Test the BC plan regularly to evaluate its performance and identify its limitations.

→ Assess the performance reports and identify limitations.

→ Update the BC plans and recovery/restart procedures to reflect regular changes within the data center.

3.1.4 Failure Analysis

3.1.4.1   Single Point of Failure

➢ A **single point of failure** refers to the failure of a component that can terminate the availability of the entire system or IT service.

➢ Fig 3.5 depicts a system setup in which an application, running on a VM, provides an interface to the client and performs I/O operations.

➢ The client is connected to the server through an IP network, the server is connected to the storage array through a FC connection, an HBA installed at the server sends or receives data to and from a storage array, and an FC switch connects the HBA to the storage port

➢ In a setup where **each component must function as required to ensure data availability,** the failure of a single physical or virtual component causes the failure of the entire data center or an application, resulting in disruption of business operations.

➢ In this example, failure of a hypervisor can affect all the running VMs and the virtual network, which are hosted on it.

➢ The can be several similar single points of failure identified in this example. A VM, a hypervisor, an HBA/NIC on the server, the physical server, the IP network, the FC switch, the storage array ports, or even the storage array could be a potential single point of failure. To avoid single points of failure, it is essential to implement a fault-tolerant mechanism.

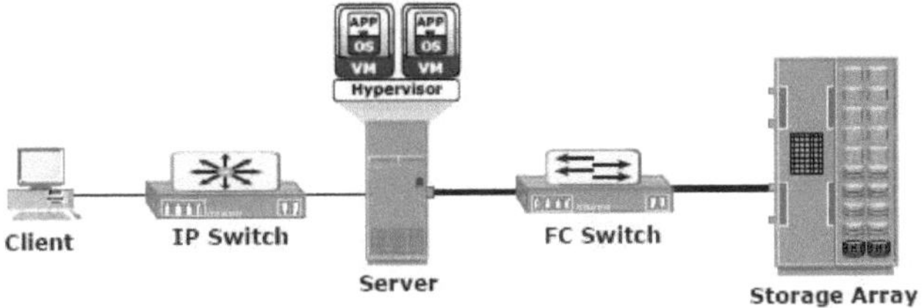

Fig 3.5: Single Point of Failure

3.1.4.2   Resolving Single Points of Failure

➢ To mitigate a single point of failure, systems are designed with redundancy, such that the system will fail only if all the components in the redundancy group fail. This ensures that the failure of a single component does not affect data availability.

➢ Data centers follow stringent guidelines to implement fault tolerance for uninterrupted information availability. Careful analysis is performed to eliminate every single point of failure.

➢ The example shown in Fig 3.6 represents all enhancements of the system shown in Fig 3.5 in the infrastructure to mitigate single points of failure:

- Configuration of redundant HBAs at a server to mitigate single HBA failure
- Configuration of NIC (network interface card) teaming at a server allows protection against single physical NIC failure. It allows grouping of two or more physical NICs and treating them as a single logical device. NIC teaming eliminates the single point of failure associated with a single physical NIC.
- Configuration of redundant switches to account for a switch failure
- Configuration of multiple storage array ports to mitigate a port failure
- RAID and hot spare configuration to ensure continuous operation in the event of disk failure
- Implementation of a redundant storage array at a remote site to mitigate local site failure
- Implementing server (or compute) clustering, a fault-tolerance mechanism whereby two or more servers in a cluster access the same set of data volumes. Clustered servers exchange a heartbeat to inform each other about their health. If one of the servers or hypervisors fails, the other server or hypervisor can take up the workload.
- Implementing a VM Fault Tolerance mechanism ensures BC in the event of a server failure. This technique creates duplicate copies of each VM on another server so that when a VM failure is detected, the duplicate VM can be used for failover. The two VMs are kept in synchronization with each other in order to perform successful failover.

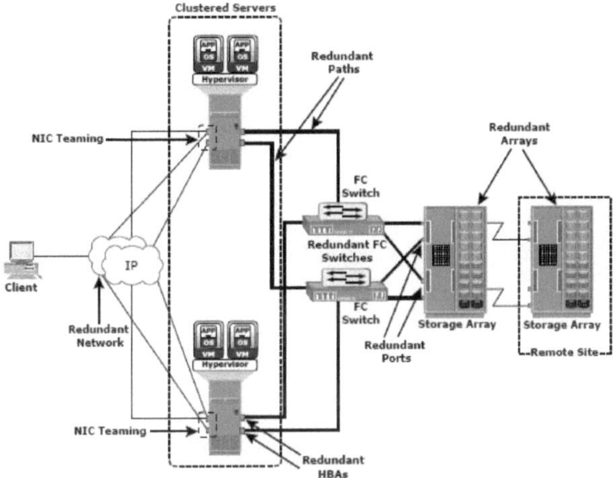

Fig 3.6: Resolving single points of failure

3.1.4.3   Multipathing Software

- Configuration of multiple paths increases the data availability through path failover. If servers are configured with one I/O path to the data there will be no access to the data if that path fails. Redundant paths eliminate the path to become single points of failure.

- Multiple paths to data also improve I/O performance through load sharing and maximize server, storage, and data path utilization.

- In practice, merely configuring multiple paths does not serve the purpose. Even with multiple paths, if one path fails, I/O will not reroute unless the system recognizes that it has an alternate path.

- Multipathing software provides the functionality to recognize and utilize alternate I/O path to data. Multipathing software also manages the load balancing by distributing I/Os to all available, active paths.

- In a virtual environment, multipathing is enabled either by using the hypervisor's built-in capability or by running a third-party software module, added to the hypervisor.

3.1.5 BC Technology Solutions

After analyzing the business impact of an outage, designing appropriate solutions to recover from a failure is the next important activity. One or more copies of the original data are maintained using any of the following strategies, so that data can be recovered and business operations can be restarted using an alternate copy:

1. **Backup:** Data backup is a predominant method of ensuring data availability. The frequency of backup is determined based on RPO, RTO, and the frequency of data changes.

2. **Storage array-based replication (local):** Data can be replicated to a separate location within the same storage array. The replica is used independently for other business operations. Replicas can also be used for restoring operations if data corruption occurs.

3. **Storage array-based replication (remote):** Data in a storage array can be replicated to another storage array located at a remote site. If the storage array is lost due to a disaster, business operations can be started from the remote storage array.

3.2   Backup and Recovery

➤ **Data Backup** is a copy of production data, created and retained for the sole purpose of recovering lost or corrupted data.

➤ Evaluating the various backup methods along with their recovery considerations and retention requirements is an essential step to implement a successful backup and recovery solution.

➤ Organizations generate and maintain large volumes of data, and most of the data is fixed content. This fixed content is rarely accessed after a period of time. Still, this data needs to be retained for several years to meet regulatory compliance.

➤ **Data archiving** is the process of moving data that is no longer actively used, from primary storage to a low-cost secondary storage. This data is retained in the secondary storage for a long term to meet regulatory requirements. This reduces the amount of data to be backed up and the time required to back up the data.

3.2.1 Backup Purpose

Backups are performed to serve three purposes: ***disaster recovery, operational recovery, and archival***. These are discussed in the following sections.

3.2.1.1   Disaster Recovery

➤ Backups are performed to address disaster recovery needs.

➤ The backup copies are used for restoring data at an alternate site when the primary site is incapacitated due to a disaster. Based on RPO and RTO requirements, organizations use different backup strategies for disaster recovery.

➤ When a tape-based backup method is used as a disaster recovery strategy, the backup tape media is shipped and stored at an offsite location. These tapes can be recalled for restoration at the disaster recovery site.

➤ Organizations with stringent RPO and RTO requirements use remote replication technology to replicate data to a disaster recovery site. Organizations can bring production systems online in a relatively short period of time if a disaster occurs.

3.2.1.2   Operational Recovery

➤ Data in the production environment changes with every business transaction and operation.

➤ Operational recovery is the use of backups to restore data if data loss or logical corruption occurs during routine processing.

➤ For example, it is common for a user to accidentally delete an important email or for a file to become corrupted, which can be restored from operational backup.

3.2.1.3   Archival

➤ Backups are also performed to address archival requirements.

➤ Traditional backups are still used by small and medium enterprises for long-term preservation of transaction records, e- mail messages, and other business records required for regulatory compliance.

Apart from addressing disaster recovery, archival, and operational requirements, backups serve as a protection against data loss due to physical damage of a storage device, software failures, or virus attacks. Backups can also be used to protect against accidents such as a deletion or intentional data destruction.

3.2.2 Backup Methods

➤ **Hot backup and cold backup** are the two methods deployed for backup. They are based on the state of the application when the backup is performed.

➤ In a **hot backup**, the application is up and running, with users accessing their data during the backup process. This method of backup is also referred to as an *online backup*.

➤ In a **cold backup**, the application is not active or shutdown during the backup process and is also called as *offline backup*.

➤ The hot backup of online production data becomes more challenging because data is actively used and changed.

➤ An open file is locked by the operating system and is not backed up during the backup process. In such situations, an *open file agent* is required to back up the open file.

➤ In database environments, the use of open file agents is not enough, because the agent should also support a consistent backup of all the database components.

➤ For example, a database is composed of many files of varying sizes occupying several file systems. To ensure a consistent database backup, all files need to be backed up in the same state. That does not necessarily mean that all files need to be backed up at the same time, but they all must be synchronized so that the database can be restored with consistency.

➤ The disadvantage associated with a hot backup is that the agents usually affect the overall application performance.

➢ Consistent backups of databases can also be done by using a cold backup. This requires the database to remain inactive during the backup. Of course, the disadvantage of a cold backup is that the database is inaccessible to users during the backup process.

➢ Hot backup is used in situations where it is not possible to shut down the database. This is facilitated by database backup agents that can perform a backup while the database is active. The disadvantage associated with a hot backup is that the agents usually affect overall application performance.

➢ A **point-in-time (PIT)** copy method is deployed in environments where the impact of downtime from a cold backup or the performance resulting from a hot backup is unacceptable. The PIT copy is created from the production volume and used as the source for the backup. This reduces the impact on the production volume.

➢ Certain attributes and properties attached to a file, such as permissions, owner, and other metadata, also need to be backed up. These attributes are as important as the data itself and must be backed up for consistency.

➢ Backup of boot sector and partition layout information is also critical for successful recovery.

➢ In a disaster recovery environment, **bare-metal recovery (BMR)** refers to a backup in which all metadata, system information, and application configurations are appropriately backed up for a full system recovery. BMR builds the base system, which includes partitioning, the file system layout, the operating system, the applications, and all the relevant configurations. BMR recovers the base system first, before starting the recovery of data files. Some BMR technologies can recover a server onto dissimilar hardware.

3.2.3 Backup Topologies

➤ Three basic topologies are used in a backup environment:

1. Direct attached backup

2. LAN based backup, and

3. SAN based backup.

➤ A **mixed topology** is also used by combining LAN based and SAN based topologies.

➤ In a **direct-attached backup**, a backup device is attached directly to the client. Only the metadata is sent to the backup server through the LAN. This configuration frees the LAN from backup traffic.

➤ The example shown in Fig 3.7 device is directly attached and dedicated to the backup client. As the environment grows, however, there will be a need for central management of all backup devices and to share the resources to optimize costs. An appropriate solution is to share the backup devices among multiple servers. Network-based topologies (LAN-based and SAN-based) provide the solution to optimize the utilization of backup devices.

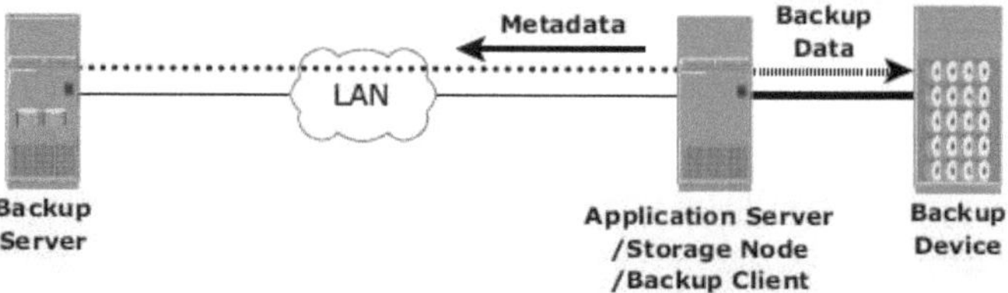

Fig 3.7: Direct-attached backup topology

➤ In **LAN-based backup**, the clients, backup server, storage node, and backup device are connected to the LAN (see Fig 3.8). The data to be backed up is transferred from the backup client (source), to the backup device (destination) over the LAN, which may affect network performance.

➤ This impact can be minimized by adopting a number of measures, such as configuring separate networks for backup and installing dedicated storage nodes for some application servers.

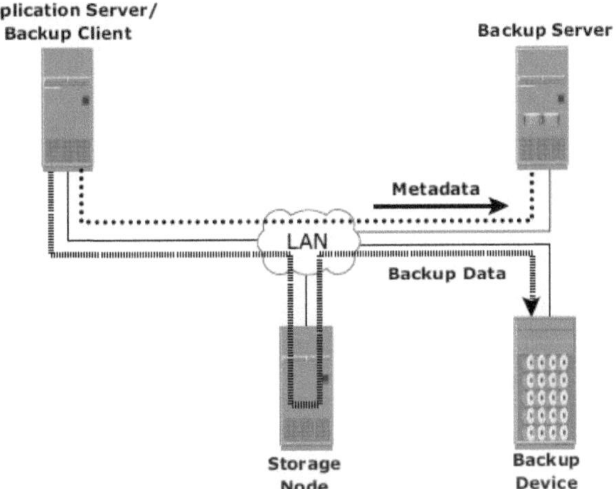

Fig 3.8: LAN-based backup topology

➤ The **SAN-based backup** is also known as the *LAN-free backup*. Fig 3.9 illustrates a SAN-based backup. The SAN-based backup topology is the most appropriate solution when a backup device needs to be shared among the clients. In this case the backup device and clients are attached to the SAN.

➤ In the example from Fig 3.9, a client sends the data to be backed up to the backup device over the SAN. Therefore, the backup data traffic is restricted to the SAN, and only the backup metadata is transported over the LAN. The volume of metadata is insignificant when compared to the production data; the LAN performance is not degraded in this configuration.

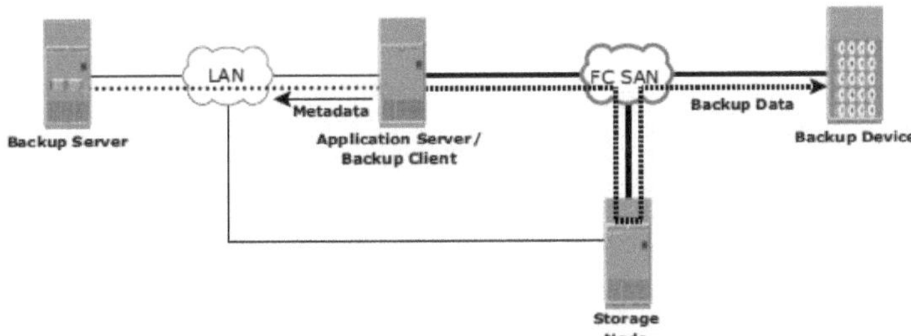

Fig 3.9: SAN-based backup topology

➤ The emergence of low-cost disks as a backup medium has enabled disk arrays to be attached to the SAN and used as backup devices. A tape backup of these data backups on the disks can be created and shipped offsite for disaster recovery and long-term retention.

> The mixed topology uses both the LAN-based and SAN-based topologies, as shown in Fig 3.10. This topology might be implemented for several reasons, including cost, server location, reduction in administrative overhead, and performance considerations.

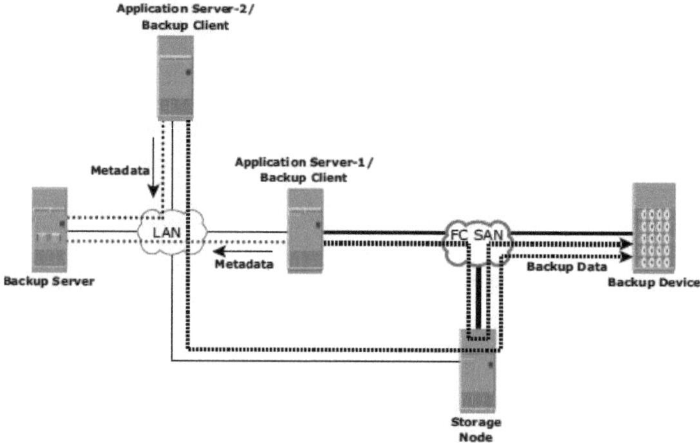

Fig 3.10: Mixed backup topology

3.2.4 Backup Technologies

> A wide range of technology solutions are currently available for backup targets.

> Tapes and disks are the two most commonly used backup media. Virtual tape libraries use disks as backup medium emulating tapes, providing enhanced backup and recovery capabilities.

3.2.4.1   Backup to Tape

> Tapes, a low-cost technology, are used extensively for backup. Tape drives are used to read/write data from/to a tape cartridge. Tape drives are referred to as sequential, or linear, access devices because the data is written or read sequentially.

> A tape cartridge is composed of magnetic tapes in a plastic enclosure.

> Tape Mounting is the process of inserting a tape cartridge into a tape drive. The tape drive has motorized controls to move the magnetic tape around, enabling the head to read or write data.

> Several types of tape cartridges are available. They vary in size, capacity, shape, number of reels, density, tape length, tape thickness, tape tracks, and supported speed.

Physical Tape Library

➤ The physical tape library provides housing and power for a number of tape drives and tape cartridges, along with a robotic arm or picker mechanism.

➤ The backup software has intelligence to manage the robotic arm and entire backup process. Fig 3-14 shows a physical tape library.

➤ *Tape drives* read and write data from and to a tape. Tape cartridges are placed in the slots when not in use by a tape drive. *Robotic arms* are used to move tapes around the library, such as moving a tape drive into a slot.

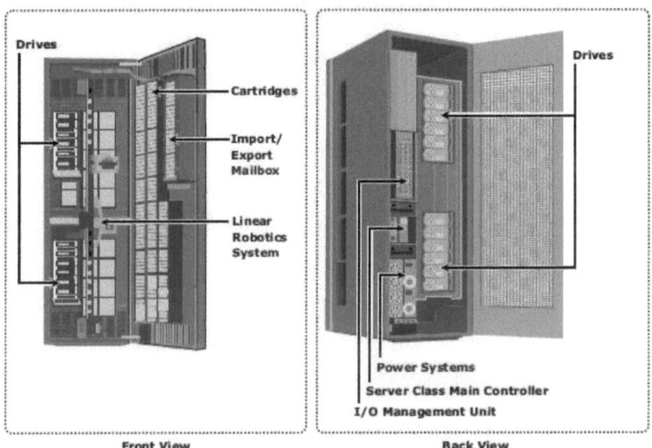

Fig 3.11: Physical tape library

➤ Another type of slot called a *mail or import/export* slot is used to add or remove tapes from the library without opening the access doors (Fig 3.11 Front View) because opening the access doors causes a library to go offline.

➤ In addition, each physical component in a tape library has an individual element address that is used as an addressing mechanism for moving tapes around the library.

➤ When a backup process starts, the robotic arm is instructed to load a tape to a tape drive. This process adds to the delay to a degree depending on the type of hardware used, but it generally takes 5 to 10 seconds to mount a tape. After the tape is mounted, additional time is spent to position the heads and validate header information. This total time is called *load to ready time*, and it can vary from several seconds to minutes.

➤ The tape drive receives backup data and stores the data in its internal buffer. This backup data is then written to the tape in blocks. During this process, it is best to ensure that the tape drive is kept busy continuously to prevent gaps between the blocks. This is accomplished by buffering the data on tape drives.

➢ The speed of the tape drives can also be adjusted to match data transfer rates.

➢ Tape drive *streaming or multiple streaming* writes data from multiple streams on a single tape to keep the drive busy. Shown in Fig 3.12, multiple streaming improves media performance, but it has an associated disadvantage. The backup data is interleaved because data from multiple streams is written on it.

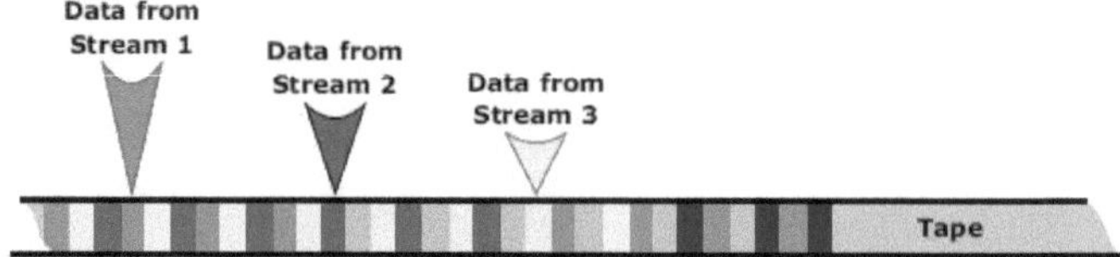

Fig 3.12: Physical tape library

➢ Many times, even the buffering and speed adjustment features of a tape drive fail to prevent the gaps, causing the *"shoe shining effect" or "backhitching."* This is the repeated back and forth motion a tape drive makes when there is an interruption in the backup data stream. This repeated back-and-forth motion not only causes a degradation of service, but also excessive wear and tear to tapes.

➢ When the tape operation finishes, the tape rewinds to the starting position and it is unmounted. The robotic arm is then instructed to move the unmounted tape back to the slot. *Rewind time* can range from several seconds to minutes.

➢ When a *restore* is initiated, the backup software identifies which tapes are required. The robotic arm is instructed to move the tape from its slot to a tape drive. If the required tape is not found in the tape library, the backup software displays a message, instructing the operator to manually insert the required tape in the tape library.

➢ When a file or a group of files require restores, the tape must move sequentially to the beginning of the data before it can start reading. This process can take a significant amount of time, especially if the required files are recorded at the end of the tape.

➢ Modern tape devices have an indexing mechanism that enables a tape to be fast forwarded to a location near the required data.

Limitations of Tape

➢ Tapes must be stored in locations with a controlled environment to ensure preservation of the media and prevent data corruption.

➢ Data access in a tape is sequential, which can slow backup and recovery operations.

➢ Physical transportation of the tapes to offsite locations also adds management overhead.

3.2.4.2   Backup to Disk

➢ Because of *increased availability,* low cost **disks** have now replaced tapes as the primary device for storing backup data because of their *performance advantages.* Backup-to-disk systems offer *ease of implementation, reduced TCO* (Total cost of ownership), and *improved quality of service.* Disks also offer *faster recovery* when compared to tapes.

➢ Backing up to disk storage systems offers clear advantages due to their inherent random access and RAID-protection capabilities.

➢ Fig 3.13 illustrates a recovery scenario comparing tape versus disk in a Microsoft Exchange environment that supports 800 users with a 75 MB mailbox size and a 60 GB database. As shown, a restore from disk took 24 minutes compared to the restore from a tape, which took 108 minutes for the same environment.

➢ Recovering from a full backup copy stored on disk and kept onsite provides the fastest recovery solution. Using a disk enables the creation of full backups more frequently, which in turn improves RPO and RTO.

➢ Backup to disk does not offer any inherent offsite capability, and is dependent on other technologies such as local and remote replication.

➢ Some backup products also require additional modules and licenses to support backup to disk, which may also require additional configuration steps, including creation of RAID groups and file system tuning. These activities are not usually performed by a backup administrator.

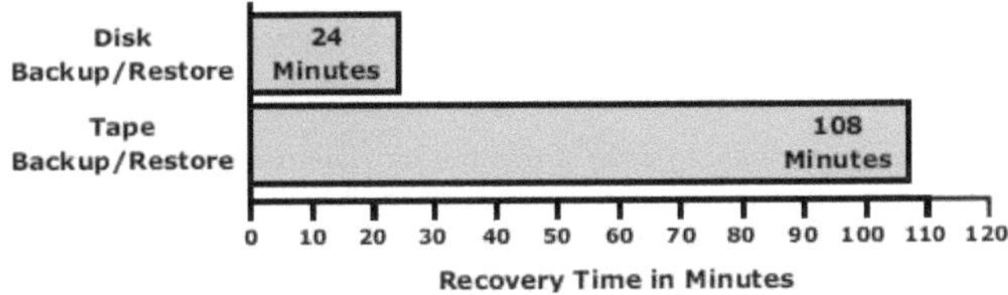

Fig 3.13: Tape versus Disk restore

3.2.4.3   Backup to Virtual Tape

➢ Virtual tapes are disk drives emulated and presented as tapes to the backup software.

➢ The key benefit of using a virtual tape is that it does not require any additional modules, configuration, or changes in the legacy backup software. This preserves the investment made in the backup software.

Virtual Tape Library

➤ A virtual tape library (VTL) has the same components as that of a physical tape library except that the majority of the components are presented as virtual resources.

➤ For the backup software, there is no difference between a physical tape library and a virtual tape library.

➤ Fig 3.14 shows a virtual tape library that uses disks as backup media. Emulation software has a database with a list of virtual tapes, and each virtual tape is assigned a portion of a LUN on the disk. A virtual tape can span multiple LUNs if required.

➤ File system awareness is not required while backing up because virtual tape solutions use raw devices.

➤ Similar to a physical tape library, a robot mount is performed when a backup process starts in a virtual tape library. However, unlike a physical tape library, where this process involves some mechanical delays, in a virtual tape library it is almost instantaneous. Even the *load to ready* time is much less than in a physical tape library.

➤ After the virtual tape is mounted and the tape drive is positioned, the virtual tape is ready to be used, and backup data can be written to it. Unlike a physical tape library, the virtual tape library is not constrained by the shoe shining effect.

➤ When the operation is complete, the backup software issues a rewind command and then the tape can be unmounted. This rewind is also instantaneous.

➤ The virtual tape is then unmounted, and the virtual robotic arm is instructed to move it back to a virtual slot.

➤ The steps to restore data are similar to those in a physical tape library, but the restore operation is instantaneous. Even though virtual tapes are based on disks, which provide random access, they still emulate the tape behavior.

➤ Virtual tape library appliances offer a number of features that are not available with physical tape libraries.

➤ Some virtual tape libraries offer *multiple emulation engines* configured in an active cluster configuration. An engine is a dedicated server with a customized operating system that makes physical disks in the VTL appear as tapes to the backup application. With this feature, one engine can pick up the virtual resources from another engine in the event of any failure.

➤ Replication over IP is available with most of the virtual tape library appliances. This feature enables virtual tapes to be replicated over an inexpensive IP network to a remote site.

> Connecting the engines of a virtual tape library appliance to a physical tape library enables the virtual tapes to be copied onto the physical tapes, which can then be sent to a vault or shipped to an offsite location.

> Using virtual tapes offers several advantages over both physical tapes and disks.

> Compared to physical tapes, virtual tapes offer better single stream performance, better reliability, and random disk access characteristics.

> Backup and restore operations benefit from the disk's random access characteristics because they are always online and provide faster backup and recovery.

> A virtual tape drive does not require the usual maintenance tasks associated with a physical tape drive, such as periodic cleaning and drive calibration.

> Compared to backup-to-disk devices, a virtual tape library offers easy installation and administration because it is preconfigured by the manufacturer.

> However, a virtual tape library is generally used only for backup purposes. In a backup-to-disk environment, the disk systems are used for both production and backup data.

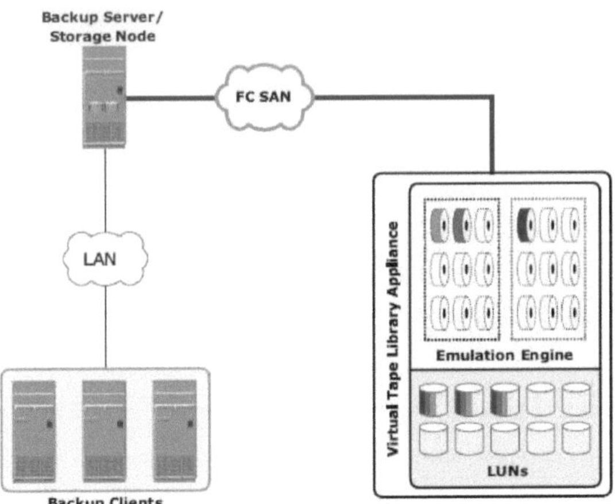

Fig 3.14: Virtual Tape Library

3.2.4.4   Backup Targets Comparison

Table 3.2 shows a comparison between various backup targets.

FEATURES	TAPE	DISK	VIRTUAL TAPE
Offsite Replication Capabilities	No	Yes	Yes
Reliability	No inherent protection methods	Yes	Yes
Performance	Subject to mechanical operations, loading time	Faster single stream	Faster single stream
Use	Backup only	Multiple (backup, production)	Backup only

Table 3.2: Backup targets comparison

3.2.5 Data Deduplication for Backup

➢ **Data deduplication** is the process of identifying and eliminating redundant data. When duplicate data is detected during backup, the data is discarded and only the pointer is created to refer the copy of the data that is already backed up.

➢ Data deduplication helps to reduce the storage requirement for backup, shorten the backup window, and remove the network burden. It also helps to store more backups on the disk and retain the data on the disk for a longer time.

3.2.5.1   Data Deduplication Methods

➢ There are two methods of deduplication: *file level* and *subfile* level.

➢ The differences exist in the amount of data reduction each method produces and the time each approach takes to determine the unique content.

➢ *File-level deduplication* (also called single-instance storage) detects and removes redundant copies of identical files. It enables storing only one copy of the file; the subsequent copies are replaced with a pointer that points to the original file.

➢ File-level deduplication is simple and fast but does not address the problem of duplicate content inside the files. For example, two 10-MB PowerPoint presentations with a difference in just the title page are not considered as duplicate files, and each file will be stored separately.

> ***Subfile deduplication*** breaks the file into smaller chunks and then uses a specialized algorithm to detect redundant data within and across the file. As a result, subfile deduplication eliminates duplicate data across files.

> There are two forms of subfile deduplication: fixed-length block and variable-length segment.

> *The fixed-length block deduplication* divides the files into fixed length blocks and uses a hash algorithm to find the duplicate data.

> Although simple in design, fixed-length blocks might miss many opportunities to discover redundant data because the block boundary of similar data might be different. Consider the addition of a person's name to a document's title page. This shifts the whole document, and all the blocks appear to have changed, causing the failure of the deduplication method to detect equivalencies.

> In *variable-length segment deduplication,* if there is a change in the segment, the boundary for only that segment is adjusted, leaving the remaining segments unchanged. This method vastly improves the ability to find duplicate data segments compared to fixed-block.

3.2.5.2   Data Deduplication Implementation

Deduplication for backup can happen at the data source or the backup target.

Source-Based Data Deduplication

> *Source-based data deduplication* eliminates redundant data at the source before it transmits to the backup device.

> Source-based data deduplication can dramatically reduce the amount of backup data sent over the network during backup processes. It provides the benefits of a shorter backup window and requires less network bandwidth. There is also a substantial reduction in the capacity required to store the backup images.

> Fig 3.15 shows source-based data deduplication.

> Source-based deduplication increases the overhead on the backup client, which impacts the performance of the backup and application running on the client.

> Source-based deduplication might also require a change of backup software if it is not supported by backup software.

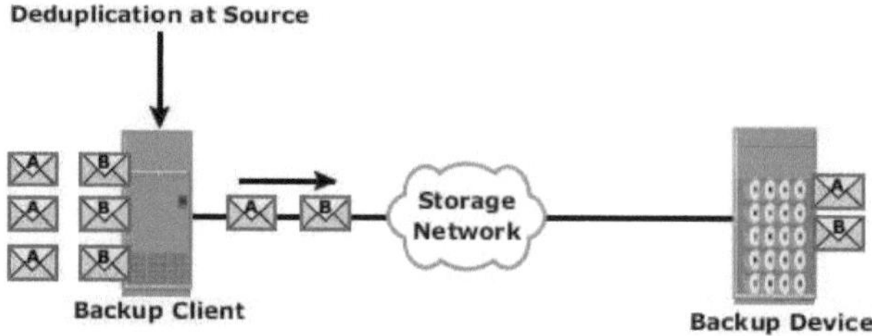

Fig 3.15: Source-based data deduplication

Target-Based Data Deduplication

➤ Target-based data deduplication is an alternative to source-based data deduplication.

➤ Target-based data deduplication occurs at the backup device, which offloads the backup client from the deduplication process.

➤ Fig 3.16 shows target-based data deduplication.

➤ In this case, the backup client sends the data to the backup device and the data is deduplicated at the backup device, either *immediately (inline)* or at a *scheduled time (post-process)*.

➤ Because deduplication occurs at the target, all the backup data needs to be transferred over the network, which increases network bandwidth requirements. Target-based data deduplication does not require any changes in the existing backup software.

➤ *Inline deduplication* performs deduplication on the backup data before it is stored on the backup device. Hence, this method reduces the storage capacity needed for the backup.

➤ Inline deduplication introduces overhead in the form of the time required to identify and remove duplication in the data. So, this method is best suited for an environment with a large backup window.

➤ *Post-process deduplication* enables the backup data to be stored or written on the backup device first and then deduplicated later.

➤ This method is suitable for situations with tighter backup windows. However, post-process deduplication requires more storage capacity to store the backup images before they are deduplicated.

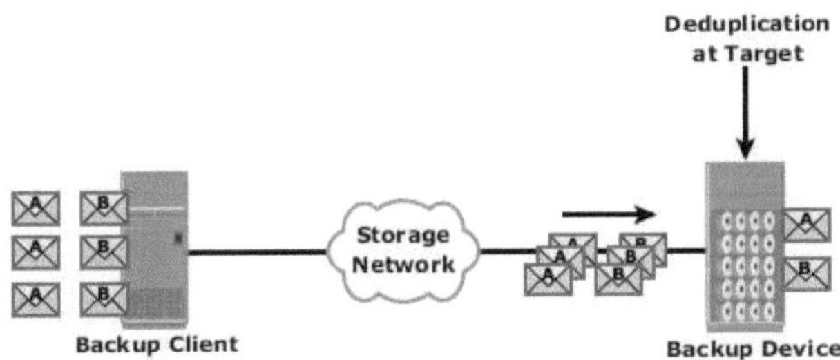

Fig 3.16: Target-based data deduplication

3.2.6 Backup in Virtualized Environments

> There are two approaches for performing a backup in a virtualized environment: the *traditional backup* approach and the *image-based* backup approach.

> In *the traditional backup* approach, a backup agent is installed either on the virtual machine (VM) or on the hypervisor.

> Fig 3.17 shows the traditional VM backup approach.

> If the backup agent is installed on a VM, the VM appears as a physical server to the agent. The backup agent installed on the VM backs up the VM data to the backup device. The agent does not capture VM files, such as the virtual BIOS file, VM swap file, logs, and configuration fi les. Therefore, for a VM restore, a user needs to manually re-create the VM and then restore data onto it.

> If the backup agent is installed on the hypervisor, the VMs appear as a set of files to the agent. So, VM files can be backed up by performing a file system backup from a hypervisor. This approach is relatively simple because it requires having the agent just on the hypervisor instead of all the VMs.

> The traditional backup method can cause high CPU utilization on the server being backed up.

> So the backup should be performed when the server resources are idle or during a low activity period on the network.

> And also allocate enough resources to manage the backup on each server when a large number of VMs are in the environment.

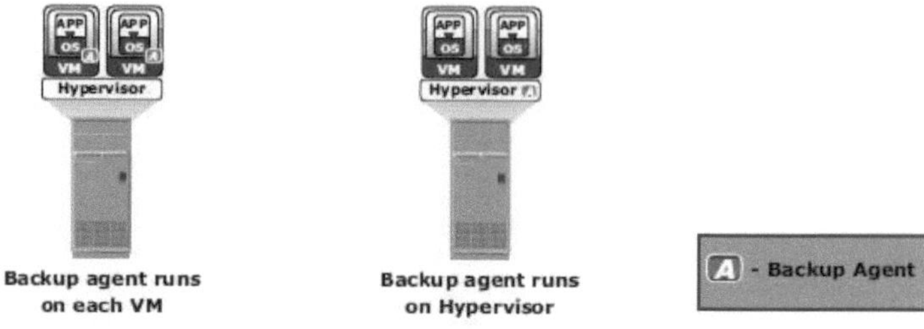

Fig 3.17: Traditional VM backup

> *Image-based backup* operates at the hypervisor level and essentially takes a snapshot of the VM.

> It creates a copy of the guest OS and all the data associated with it (snapshot of VM disk files), including the VM state and application configurations. The backup is saved as a single file called an *"image,"* and this image is mounted on the separate physical machine–proxy server, which acts as a backup client.

> The backup software then backs up these image files normally. (see Fig 3.18).

> This effectively offloads the backup processing from the hypervisor and transfers the load on the proxy server, thereby reducing the impact to VMs running on the hypervisor.

> Image-based backup enables quick restoration of a VM.

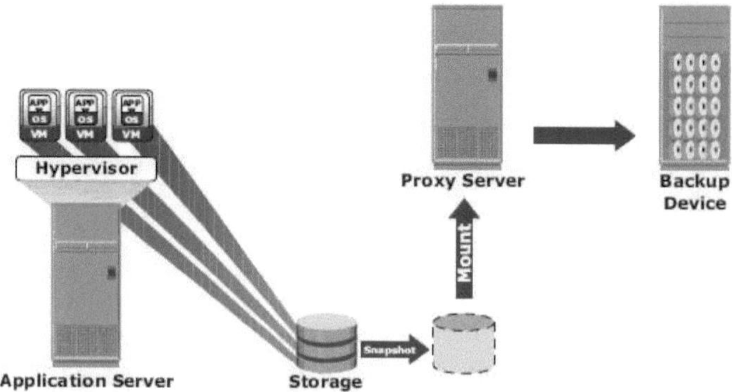

Fig 3.18: Image-based backup

CLOUD COMPUTING CHARACTERISTICS AND BENEFITS

4.1 Drivers for cloud computing

- ➢ Business requirements

  - Transformation of IT processes to achieve more with less

  - better agility and higher availability at reduced expenditures

  - Reduced time-to-market

  - Accelerated pace of innovation

- ➢ IT challenges to meet business requirements are:

  - Serving customers worldwide round the clock, refreshing technology quickly, faster provisioning of IT resources-all at reduced cost.

- ➢ These challenges are addressed with the emergence of cloud computing.

4.2 Definition

Cloud computing is a model for enabling ubiquitous, convenient, on-demand network access to a shared pool of configurable computing resources (e.g., networks, servers, storage, applications, and services) that can be rapidly provisioned and released with minimal management effort or service provider interaction.

4.3 Characteristics of Cloud Computing

Cloud infrastructure should have five essential characteristics:

- ➢ **On-demand self-service:** A consumer can unilaterally provision computing capabilities, such as server time and network storage, as needed, automatically without requiring human interaction with each service provider.

     A cloud service provider publishes a service catalogue, which contains information about all cloud services available to consumers. The service catalogue includes information about service attributes, prices, and request processes. Consumers view the service catalogue via a web-based user interface and use it to request for a service. Consumers can either leverage the "ready-to-use" services or change a few service parameters to customize the services.

- ➢ **Broad network access:** Capabilities are available over the network and accessed through standard mechanisms that promote use by heterogeneous thin or thick client platforms (for example, mobile phones, tablets, laptops, and workstations).

- ➢ **Resource pooling:** The provider's computing resources are pooled to serve multiple consumers using a multitenant model, with different physical and virtual resources dynamically assigned and reassigned according to consumer demand. There is a sense of location independence in that the customer generally has no control or knowledge over the exact location of the provided resources but may be able to specify location at a higher level of abstraction (for example, country, state, or data center). Examples of resources include storage, processing, memory, and network bandwidth.

- ➢ **Rapid elasticity:** Capabilities can be elastically provisioned and released, in some cases automatically, to scale rapidly outward and inward commensurate with demand. To the consumer, the capabilities available for provisioning

- ➢ **Measured service:** Cloud systems automatically control and optimize resource use by leveraging a metering capability at some level of abstraction appropriate to the type of service (for example, storage, processing, bandwidth, and active user accounts). Resource usage can be monitored, controlled, and reported, providing transparency for both the provider and consumer of the utilized service.

4.4 Benefits of cloud computing

Benefits	Description
Reduced IT cost	• Reduces the up-front capital expenditure (CAPEX)
Business agility	• Provides the ability to deploy new resources quickly • Enables businesses to reduce time-to-market
Flexible scaling	• Enables consumers to scale up, scale down, scale out, or scale in the demand for computing resources easily • Consumers can unilaterally and automatically scale computing resources
High availability	• Ensures resource availability at varying levels, depending on consumer's policy and priority

Fig 4.1: Cloud enabling technologies

4.5 Cloud Enabling Technologies

Technologies	Description
Grid computing	• Form of distributed computing • Enables resources of numerous computers in a network to work on a single task at the same time
Utility computing	• Service provisioning model that offers computing resources as a metered service
Virtualization	• Abstracts physical characteristics of IT resources from resource users • Enables resource pooling and creating virtual resources from pooled resources
Service-oriented architecture (SOA)	• Provides a set of services that can communicate with each other

Fig 4.2 : Cloud enabling Technologies

4.6 Cloud Service Models

Cloud service offerings are classified primarily into three models:
- Infrastructure-as-a-Service (IaaS),
- Platform-as-a-Service (PaaS),
- Software-as-a-Service (SaaS).

4.6.1 Infrastructure-as-a-Service

➢ The capability provided to the consumer is to provision processing, storage, networks, and other fundamental computing resources where the consumer is able to deploy and run arbitrary software, which can include operating systems and applications.

➢ The consumer does not manage or control the underlying cloud infrastructure but has control over operating systems and deployed applications; and possibly limited control of select networking components (for example, host firewalls).

➢ IaaS is the base layer of the cloud services stack (see Fig 4.3[a]). It serves as the foundation for both the SaaS and PaaS layers.

➢ Amazon Elastic Compute Cloud (Amazon EC2) is an example of IaaS that provides scalable compute capacity, on-demand, in the cloud. It enables consumers to leverage Amazon's massive computing infrastructure with no up-front capital investment.

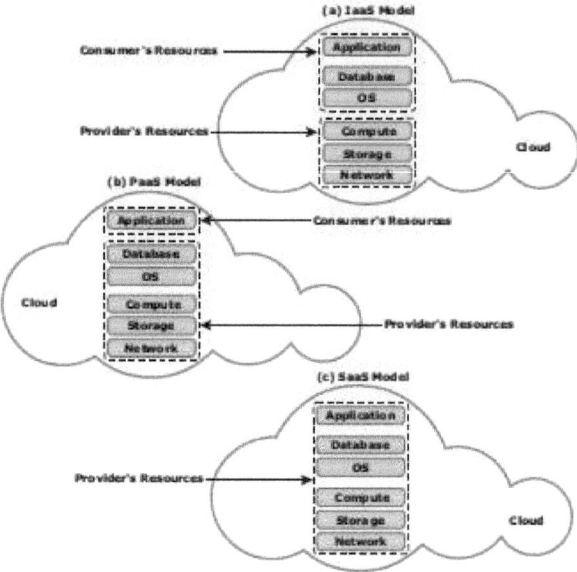

Fig 4.3 IaaS, PaaS, and SaaS models

4.6.2 Platform-as-a-Service

- ➤ The capability provided to the consumer is to deploy onto the cloud infrastructure consumer-created or acquired applications created using programming languages, libraries, services, and tools supported by the provider.
- ➤ The consumer does not manage or control the underlying cloud infrastructure including network, servers, operating systems, or storage, but has control over the deployed applications and possibly confi guration settings for the application-hosting environment. (See Fi 4.3 [b]).
- ➤ PaaS is also used as an application development environment, offered as a service by the cloud service provider.
- ➤ The consumer may use these platforms to code their applications and then deploy the applications on the cloud.
- ➤ Because the workload to the deployed applications varies, the scalability of

computing resources is usually guaranteed by the computing platform, transparently.

4.6.3 Software-as-a-Service

- The capability provided to the consumer is to use the provider's applications running on a cloud infrastructure.
- The applications are accessible from various client devices through either a thin client interface, such as a web browser (for example, web-based e-mail), or a program interface.
- The consumer does not manage or control the underlying cloud infrastructure including network, servers, operating systems, storage, or even individual application capabilities, with the possible exception of limited user-specifi c application configuration settings. (Fig 4.3[c]).
- In a SaaS model, applications, such as customer relationship management (CRM), e-mail, and instant messaging (IM), are offered as a service by the cloud service providers.
- The cloud service providers exclusively manage the required computing infrastructure and software to support these services
- . The consumers may be allowed to change a few application configuration settings to customize the applications.
- EMC Mozy is an example of SaaS. Consumers can leverage the Mozy console to perform automatic, secured, online backup and recovery of their data with ease. Salesforce.com is a provider of SaaS-based CRM applications, such as Sales Cloud and Service Cloud.Google App Engine and Microsoft Windows Azure Platform are examples of PaaS.

4.7 Cloud Deployment Models

Cloud computing is classified into four deployment models : public, private, community, and hybrid — which provide the basis for how cloud infrastructures are constructed and consumed.

4.7.1 Public Cloud

- In a public cloud model, the cloud infrastructure is provisioned for open use by the general public. It may be owned, managed, and operated by a business, academic, or government organization, or some combination of them.

- ➢ It exists on the premises of the cloud provider.
- ➢ Consumers use the cloud services offered by the providers via the Internet and pay metered usage charges or subscription fees.
- ➢ An advantage of the public cloud is its low capital cost with enormous scalability. However, for consumers, these benefits come with certain risks: no control over the resources in the cloud, the security of confidential data, network performance, and interoperability issues.
- ➢ Popular public cloud service providers are Amazon, Google, and Salesforce.com.
- ➢ Fig 4.2 shows a public cloud that provides cloud services to organizations and individuals.

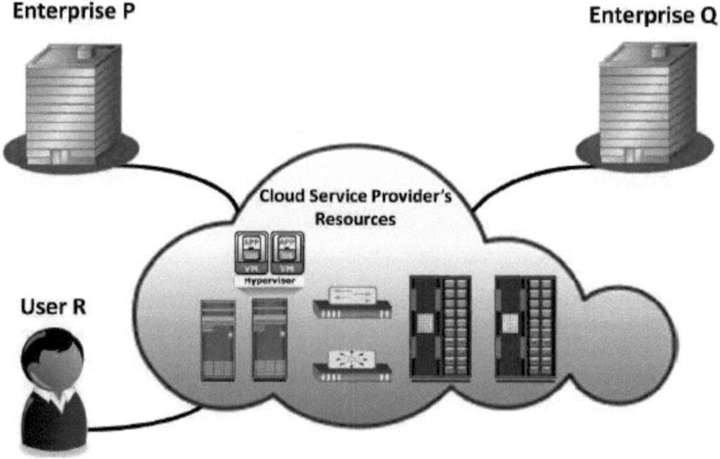

Fig 4.4 Public cloud

4.7.2 Private Cloud

- ➢ In a private cloud model, the cloud infrastructure is provisioned for exclusive use by a single organization comprising multiple consumers (for example, business units).
- ➢ It may be owned, managed, and operated by the organization, a third party, or some combination of them, and it may exist on or off premises.

➢ Following are two variations to the private cloud model:

1. **On-premise private cloud:** The on-premise private cloud, also known as internal cloud, is hosted by an organization within its own data centers (see Fig 4.5[a]). This model enables organizations to standardize their cloud service management processes and security, although this model has limitations in terms of size and resource scalability.

2. **Externally hosted private cloud:** This type of private cloud is hosted external to an organization (see Fig 4.4[b]) and is managed by a third party organization. The third-party organization facilitates an exclusive cloud environment for a specifi c organization with full guarantee of privacy and confi dentiality.

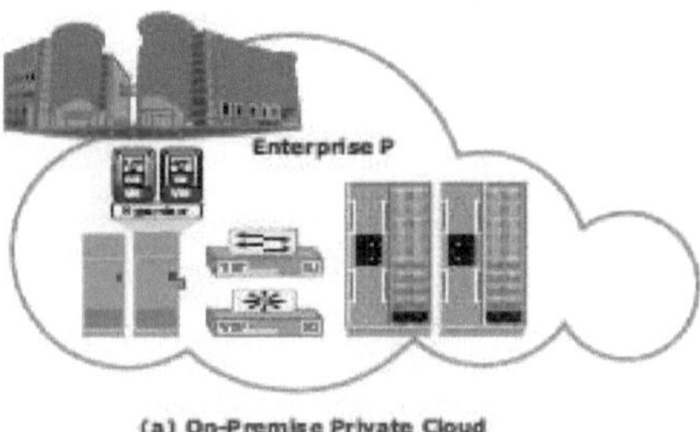

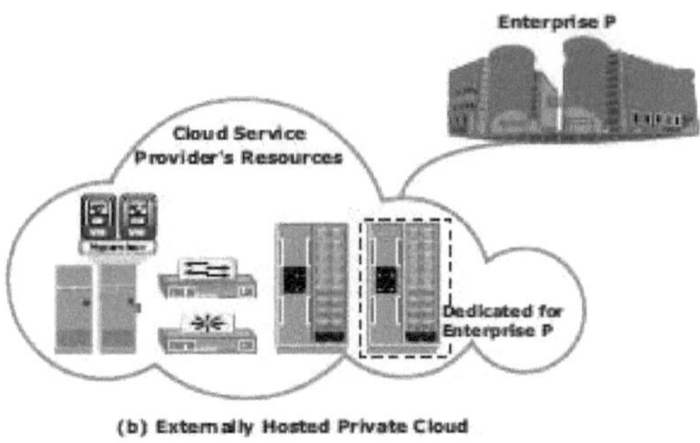

Fig 4.4 On-premise and externally hosted private clouds

4.7.3 Community Cloud

➢ In a community cloud model, the cloud infrastructure is provisioned for exclusive use by a specific community of consumers from organizations that have shared concerns.

➢ It may be owned, managed, and operated by one or more of the organizations in the community, a third party, or some combination of them, and it may exist on or off premises. (Fig 4.5).

➤ In a community cloud, the costs spread over to fewer consumers than a public cloud. Hence, this option is more expensive but might offer a higher level of privacy, security, and compliance.

➤ The community cloud also offers organizations access to a vast pool of resources compared to the private cloud.

➤ An example in which a community cloud could be useful is government agencies. If various agencies within the government operate under similar guidelines, they could all share the same infrastructure and lower their individual agency's investment.

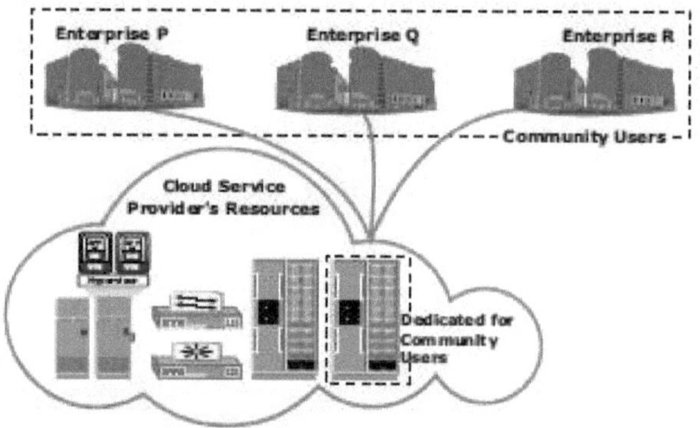

Fig 4.5 Community cloud

4.7.4 Hybrid Cloud

➤ In a hybrid cloud model, the cloud infrastructure is a composition of two or more distinct cloud infrastructures (private, community, or public) that remain unique entities, but are bound together by standardized or proprietary technology that enables data and application portability (for example, cloud bursting for load balancing between clouds).

➤ The hybrid model allows an organization to deploy less critical applications and data to the public cloud, leveraging the scalability and cost-effectiveness of the public cloud.

➤ The organization's mission-critical applications and data remain on the private cloud that provides greater security. Fig 4.6 shows an example of a hybrid cloud.

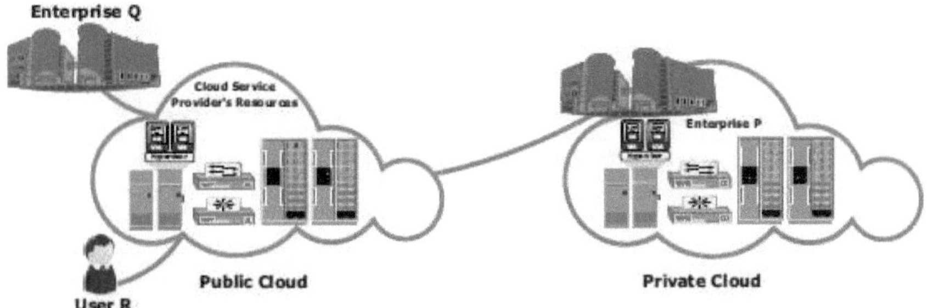

Fig 4.6 Hybrid cloud

4.8 Cloud Computing Infrastructure

A cloud computing infrastructure is the collection of hardware and software that enables the five essential characteristics of cloud computing. Cloud computing infrastructure usually consists of the following layers:

- ✓ Physical infrastructure
- ✓ Virtual infrastructure
- ✓ Applications and platform software
- ✓ Cloud management and service creation tools

The resources of these layers are aggregated and coordinated to provide cloud services to the consumers (see Fig 4.6).

4.8.1 Physical infrastructure

- ➤ The physical infrastructure consists of physical computing resources, which include physical servers, storage systems, and networks.
- ➤ Physical servers are connected to each other, to the storage systems, and to the clients via networks, such as IP, FC SAN, IP SAN, or FCoE networks.
- ➤ Cloud service providers may use physical computing resources from one or more data centers to provide services.
- ➤ If the computing resources are distributed across multiple data centers, connectivity must be established among them.

- ➢ The connectivity enables the data centers in different locations to work as a single large data center.
- ➢ This enables migration of business applications and data across data centers and provisioning cloud services using the resources from multiple data centers.

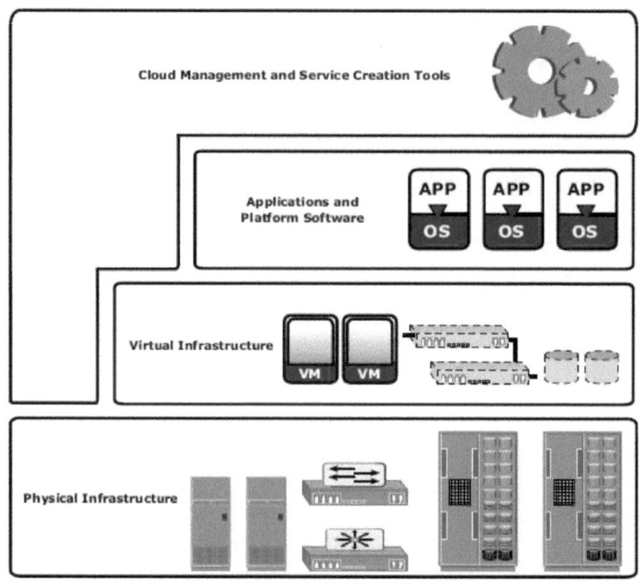

Fig 4.7 Cloud infrastructure layers

4.8.2 Virtual Infrastructure

- ➢ Cloud service providers employ virtualization technologies to build a virtual infrastructure layer on the top of the physical infrastructure.
- ➢ Virtualization enables fulfilling some of the cloud characteristics, such as resource pooling and rapid elasticity.
- ➢ It also helps reduce the cost of providing the cloud services.
- ➢ Some cloud service providers may not have completely virtualized their physical infrastructure yet, but they are adopting virtualization for better efficiency and optimization.
- ➢ Virtualization abstracts physical computing resources and provides a consolidated

view of the resource capacity.

➤ The consolidated resources are managed as a single entity called a resource pool.

➤ For example, a resource pool might group CPUs of physical servers within a cluster.

➤ The capacity of the resource pool is the sum of the power of all CPUs (for example, 10,000 megahertz) available in the cluster.

➤ In addition to the CPU pool, the virtual infrastructure includes other types of resource pools, such as memory pool, network pool, and storage pool.

➤ Apart from resource pools, the virtual infrastructure also includes identity pools, such as VLAN ID pools and VSAN ID pools.

➤ The number of each type of pool and the pool capacity depend on the cloud service provider's requirement to create different cloud services.

➤ Virtual infrastructure also includes virtual computing resources, such as virtual machines, virtual storage volumes, and virtual networks.

➤ These resources obtain capacities, such as CPU power, memory, network bandwidth, and storage space from the resource pools.

➤ Virtual networks are created using network identifiers, such as VLAN IDs and VSAN IDs from the respective identity pools.

➤ Virtual computing resources are used for creating cloud infrastructure services.

4.8.3 Applications and Platform Software

➤ This layer includes a suite of business applications and platform software, such as the OS and database.

➤ Platform software provides the environment on which business applications run.

➤ Applications and platform software are hosted on virtual machines to create SaaS and PaaS. For SaaS, both the application and platform software are provided by cloud service providers.

➤ In the case of PaaS, only the platform software is provided by cloud service providers; consumers export their applications to the cloud.

4.9 Cloud Adoption Considerations

Following are some key considerations for cloud adoption:

- ➢ **Selection of a deployment model:** Risk versus convenience is a key consideration for deciding on a cloud adoption strategy. This consideration also forms the basis for choosing the right cloud deployment model. A public cloud is usually preferred by individuals and start-up businesses. The tier 1applications should run on the private cloud, whereas less critical applications such as backup, archive, and testing can be deployed in the public cloud.

- ➢ **Application suitability:** Not all applications are good candidates for a public cloud. If an application workload is network traffi c-intensive, its performance might not be optimal if deployed in the public cloud. Also if the application communicates with other data center resources or applications, it might experience performance issues.

- ➢ **Financial advantage:** A careful analysis of financial benefits provides a clear picture about the cost-savings in adopting the cloud. The analysis should compare both the Total Cost of Ownership (TCO) and the Return on Investment (ROI) in the cloud and noncloud environment and identify the potential cost benefit. While calculating TCO and ROI, organizations and individuals should consider the expenditure to deploy and maintain their own infrastructure versus cloud-adoption costs.

- ➢ **Selection of a cloud service provider:** The selection of the provider is important for a public cloud. Consumers need to fi nd out how long and how well the provider has been delivering the services. They also need to determine how easy it is to add or terminate cloud services with the service provider. The consumer should know how easy it is to move to another provider, when required. They must assess how the provider fulfills the security, legal, and privacy requirements. They should also check whether the provider offers good customer service support.

- ➢ **Service-level agreement (SLA):** Cloud service providers typically mention quality of service (QoS) attributes such as throughput and uptime, along with cloud services. The QoS attributes are generally part of an SLA, which is the service contract between the provider and the consumers. The SLA serves as the foundation for the expected level of service between the consumer and the provider. Before adopting the cloud services, consumers should check whether the QoS attributes meet their requirements.

UNIT-V

SECURING AND MANAGING STORAGE INFRASTRUCTURE

5.1 Information Security Framework

The basic information security framework is built to achieve four security goals: confidentiality, integrity, and availability (CIA), along with accountability. This framework incorporates all security standards, procedures, and controls, required to mitigate threats in the storage infrastructure environment.

> **Confidentiality:** Provides the required secrecy of information and ensures that only authorized users have access to data. This requires authentication of users who need to access information.

> **Integrity:** Ensures that the information is unaltered. Ensuring integrity requires detection of and protection against unauthorized alteration or deletion of information. Ensuring integrity stipulates measures such as error detection and correction for both data and systems.

> **Availability**: This ensures that authorized users have reliable and timely access to systems, data, and applications residing on these systems. Availability requires protection against unauthorized deletion of data and denial of service. Availability also implies that sufficient resources are available to provide a service.

> **Accountability service**: Refers to accounting for all the events and operations that take place in the data center infrastructure. The accountability service maintains a log of events that can be audited or traced later for the purpose of security.

5.2 Risk Triad

Risk triad defines risk in terms of threats, assets, and vulnerabilities. They are considered from the perspective of risk identification and control analysis.

5.2.1 Assets

> Information is one of the most important assets for any organization. Other assets include hardware, software, and other infrastructure components required to access the information.

- To protect these assets, organizations must develop a set of parameters to ensure the availability of the resources to authorized users and trusted networks. These parameters apply to storage resources, network infrastructure, and organizational policies.
- Security methods have two objectives.
    - The first objective is to ensure that the network is easily accessible to authorized users. It should also be reliable and stable under disparate environmental conditions and volumes of usage.
    - The second objective is to make it difficult for potential attackers to access and compromise the system.
- The security methods should provide adequate protection against unauthorized access, viruses, worms, trojans, and other malicious software programs.
- Security measures should also include options to encrypt critical data and disable unused services to minimize the number of potential security gaps.
- The security method must ensure that updates to the operating system and other software are installed regularly

5.2.2 Security Threats

- Threats are the potential attacks that can be carried out on an IT infrastructure.
- Attacks can be classified as active or passive.
    - *Passive attacks* are attempts to gain unauthorized access into the system. They pose threats to confidentiality of information.
    - *Active attacks* include data modification, denial of service (DoS), and repudiation attacks. They pose threats to data integrity, availability, and accountability. **Denial of service (DoS)** attacks prevent legitimate users from accessing resources and services. **Repudiation** is an attack against the accountability of information. It attempts to provide false information by either impersonating someone or denying that an event or a transaction has taken place.

5.2.3 Vulnerabilities

- The paths that provide access to information are often vulnerable to potential attacks.
- Each of the paths may contain various access points, which provide different levels of access to the storage resources.

➢ It is important to implement adequate security controls at all the access points on an access path.

➢ Implementing security controls at each access point of every access path is known as defense in depth.

➢ Attack surface, attack vector, and work factor are the three factors to consider when assessing the extent to which an environment is vulnerable to security threats.

  o An **Attack surface** refers to the various entry points that an attacker can use to launch an attack.

  o An **attack vector** is a step or a series of steps necessary to complete an attack.

  o **Work factor** refers to the amount of time and effort required to exploit an attack vector.

5.3 Storage Security Domains

➢ To identify the threats that apply to a storage network, access paths to data storage can be categorized into three security domains: application access, management access, and backup, replication, and archive.

➢ Fig 5.1 depicts the three security domains of a storage system environment.

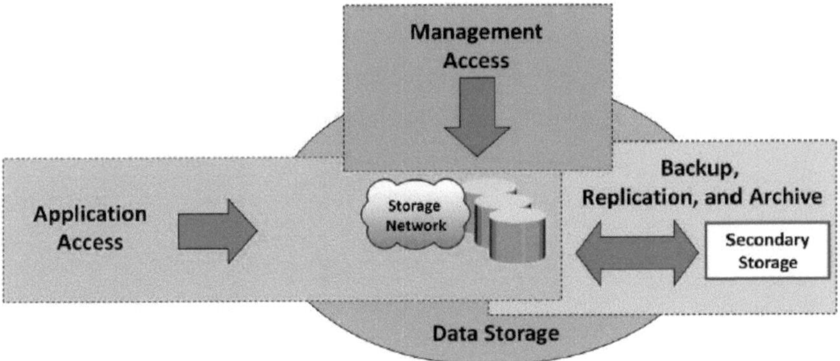

Fig 5.1: Storage security domains

➢ The first security domain involves application access to the stored data through the storage network.

➢ The second security domain includes management access to storage and interconnect devices and to the data residing on those devices. This domain is primarily accessed by storage administrators who configure and manage the environment.

➢ The third domain consists of backup, replication, and archive access. Along with the access points in this domain, the backup media also needs to be secured.

5.3.1 Securing the Application Access Domain

➢ The application access domain may include only those applications that access the data through the file system or a database interface.

➢ An important step to secure the application access domain is to identify the threats in the environment and appropriate controls that should be applied.

➢ Implementing physical security is also an important consideration to prevent media theft.

➢ Fig 5.2 shows application access in a storage networking environment.

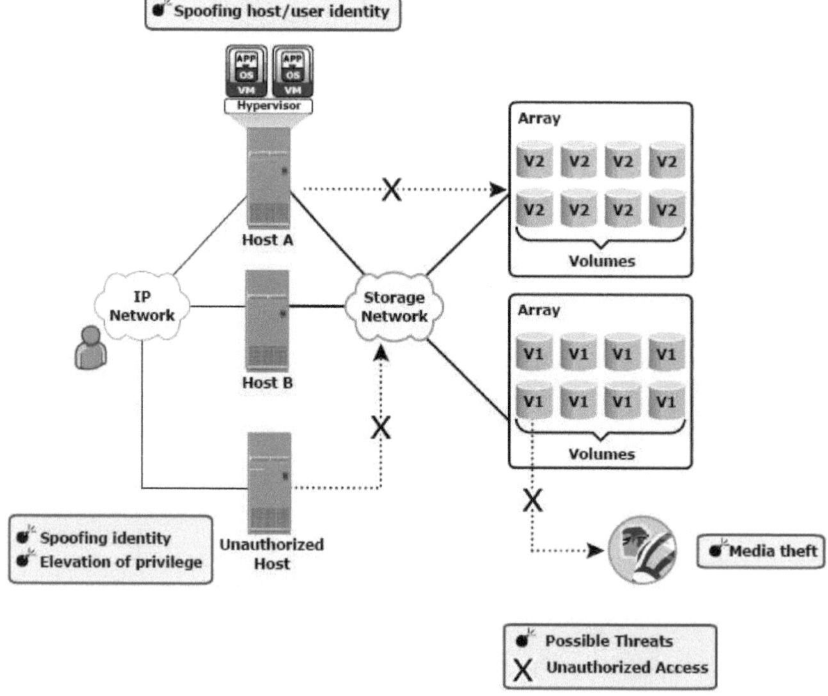

Fig 5.2: Security threats in an application access domain

> Host A can access all V1 volumes; host B can access all V2 volumes. These volumes are classified according to the access level, such as confidential, restricted, and public.

> Some of the possible threats in this scenario could be host A spoofing the identity or elevating to the privileges of host B to gain access to host B's resources. Another threat could be that an unauthorized host gains access to the network; the attacker on this host may try to spoof the identity of another host and tamper with the data, snoop the network, or execute a DoS attack.

> Also any form of media theft could also compromise security. These threats can pose several serious challenges to the network security; therefore, they need to be addressed.

5.3.2 Securing the Management Access Domain

> Management access, whether monitoring, provisioning, or managing storage resources, is associated with every device within the storage network.

> Most management software supports some form of CLI, system management console, or a web-based interface. Implementing appropriate controls for securing storage management applications is important because the damage that can be caused by using these applications can be far more extensive.

> Fig 5.3 depicts a storage networking environment in which production hosts are connected to a SAN fabric and are accessing production storage array A, which is connected to remote storage array B for replication purposes. This configuration has a storage management platform on Host A.

> A possible threat in this environment is an unauthorized host spoofing the user or host identity to manage the storage arrays or network. For example, an unauthorized host may gain management access to remote array B.

> Providing management access through an external network increases the potential for an unauthorized host or switch to connect to that network. In such circumstances, implementing appropriate security measures prevents certain types of remote communication from occurring.

> Using secure communication channels, such as Secure Shell (SSH) or Secure Sockets Layer (SSL)/Transport Layer Security (TLS), provides effective protection against these threats.

> Event log monitoring helps to identify unauthorized access and unauthorized changes to the infrastructure.

> The administrator's identity and role should be secured against any spoofing attempts so that an attacker cannot manipulate the entire storage array and cause intolerable data loss by reformatting storage media or making data resources unavailable.

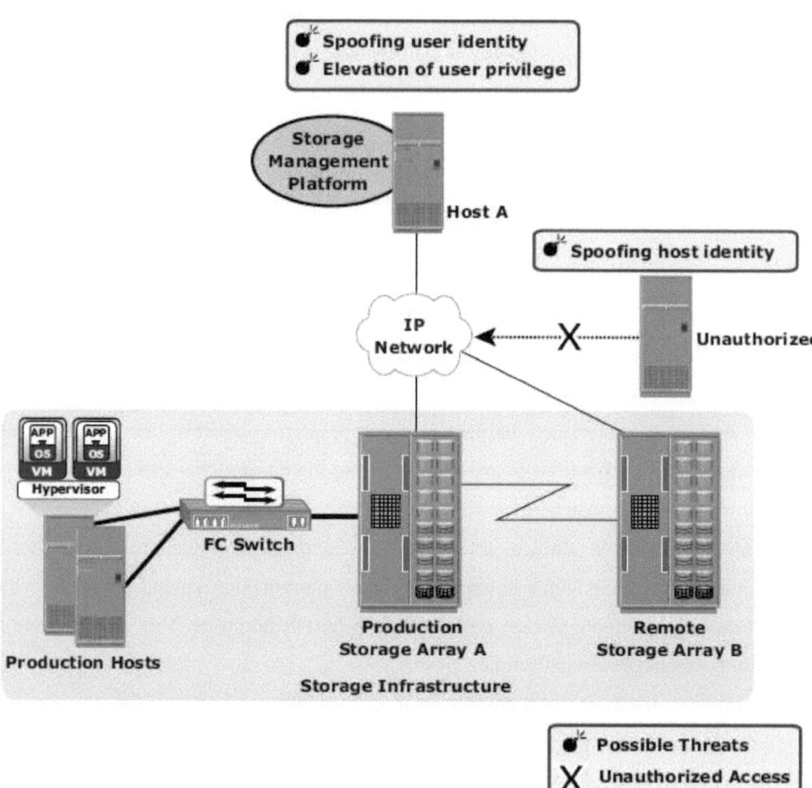

5.3.3 Securing Backup, Replication and Archive

> Backup, replication, and archive is the third domain that needs to be secured against an attack.

> A backup involves copying the data from a storage array to backup media, such as tapes or disks.

> Securing backup is complex and is based on the backup software that accesses the

storage arrays.

➤ It also depends on the configuration of the storage environments at the primary and secondary sites, especially with remote backup solutions performed directly on a remote tape device or using array-based remote replication.

➤ Organizations must ensure that the disaster recovery (DR) site maintains the same level of security for the backed up data.

➤ Protecting the backup, replication, and archive infrastructure requires addressing several threats, including spoofing the legitimate identity of a DR site, tampering with data, network snooping, DoS attacks, and media theft. Such threats represent potential violations of integrity, confidentiality, and availability.

➤ Fig 5.4 illustrates a generic remote backup design whereby data on a storage array is replicated over a DR network to a secondary storage at the DR site.

➤ The physical threat of a backup tape being lost, stolen, or misplaced, especially if the tapes contain highly confi dential information, is another type of threat. Backup-to-tape applications are vulnerable to severe security implications if they do not encrypt data while backing it up.

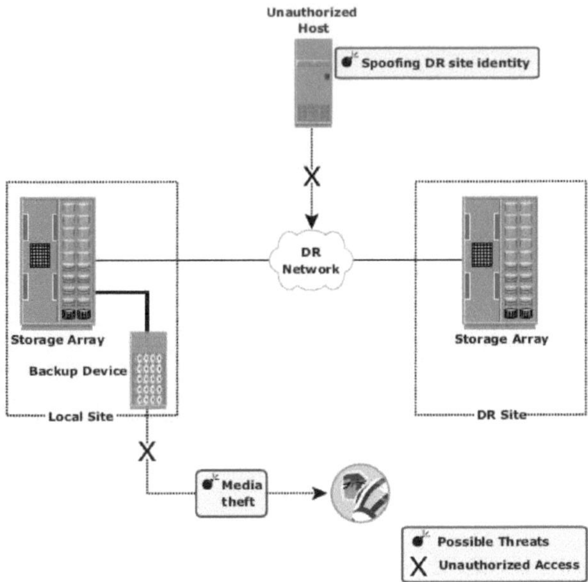

Fig 5.4: Security threats in a backup, replication, and archive environment

5.4 Security solutions for FC-SAN, IP-SAN, NAS Environment

5.4.1 FC-SAN

- ➢ Traditional FC SANs have an inherent security advantage over IP-based networks.
- ➢ An FC SAN is configured as an isolated private environment with fewer nodes than an IP network.

FC SAN Security Architecture

- ➢ Storage networking environments are a potential target for unauthorized access, theft, and misuse because of the vastness and complexity of these environments. Therefore, security strategies are based on the **defense in depth** concept, which recommends multiple integrated layers of security. This ensures that the failure of one security control will not compromise the assets under protection.
- ➢ Fig 5.5 illustrates various levels (zones) of a storage networking environment that must be secured and the security measures that can be deployed.

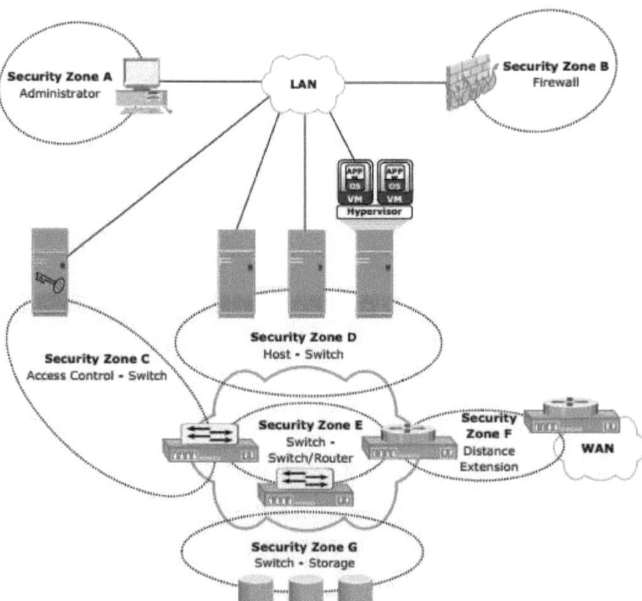

Fig 5.5: FC SAN security architecture

➤ Table 5.1 provides a comprehensive list of protection strategies that must be implemented in various security zones. Some of the security mechanisms listed in Table 5.1 are not specific to SAN but are commonly used data center techniques. For example, two-factor authentication is implemented widely; in a simple implementation it requires the use of a username/password and an additional security component such as a smart card for authentication.

Table 5.1 : list of protection strategies

SECURITY ZONES	PROTECTION STRATEGIES
Zone A (Authentication at the Management Console)	(a) Restrict management LAN access to authorized users (lock down MAC addresses); (b) implement VPN tunneling for secure remote access to the management LAN; and (c) use two-factor authentication for network access.
Zone B (Firewall)	Block inappropriate traffic by (a) filtering out addresses that should not be allowed on your LAN; and (b) screening for allowable protocols, block ports that are not in use.
Zone C (Access Control-Switch)	Authenticate users/administrators of FC switches using Remote Authentication Dial In User Service (RADIUS), DH-CHAP (Diffie-Hellman Challenge Handshake Authentication Protocol), and so on.

SECURITY ZONES	PROTECTION STRATEGIES
Zone D (Host to switch)	Restrict Fabric access to legitimate hosts by (a) implementing ACLs: Known HBAs can connect on specific switch ports only; and (b) implementing a secure zoning method, such as port zoning (also known as hard zoning).
Zone E (Switch to Switch/Switch to Router)	Protect traffic on fabric by (a) using E_Port authentication; (b) encrypting the traffic in transit; and (c) implementing FC switch controls and port controls.
Zone F (Distance Extension)	Implement encryption for in-flight data (a) FC-SP for long-distance FC extension; and (b) IPSec for SAN extension via FCIP.
Zone G (Switch to Storage)	Protect the storage arrays on your SAN via (a) WWPN-based LUN masking; and (b) S_ID locking: masking based on source FC address.

Basic SAN Security Mechanisms

➢ LUN masking and zoning, switch-wide and fabric-wide access control, RBAC, and logical partitioning of a fabric (Virtual SAN) are the most commonly used SAN security methods.

LUN Masking and Zoning

➢ LUN masking and zoning are the basic SAN security mechanisms used to protect against unauthorized access to storage.

➢ The standard implementations of LUN masking on storage arrays mask the LUNs presented to a frontend storage port based on the WWPNs of the source HBAs.

➢ A stronger variant of LUN masking may sometimes be offered whereby masking can be done on basis of source FC addresses. It offers a mechanism to lock down the FC address of a given node port to its WWN.

➢ WWPN zoning is the preferred choice in security-conscious environments.

Securing Switch Ports

➢ Apart from zoning and LUN masking, additional security mechanisms, such as port binding, port lockdown, port lockout, and persistent port disable, can be implemented on switch ports.

➢ **Port binding** limits the number of devices that can attach to a particular switch port and allows only the corresponding switch port to connect to a node for fabric access. Port binding mitigates but does not eliminate WWPN spoofing.

➢ **Port lockdown** and **port lockout** restrict a switch port's type of initialization. Typical variants of port lockout ensure that the switch port cannot function as an E_Port and cannot be used to create an ISL, such as a rogue switch. Some variants ensure that the port role is restricted to only FL_Port, F_Port, E_Port, or a combination of these.

➢ **Persistent port** disable prevents a switch port from being enabled even after a switch reboot.

Switch-Wide and Fabric-Wide Access Control

➢ As organizations grow their SANs locally or over longer distances, there is a greater need to effectively manage SAN security.

➢ Network security can be configured on the FC switch by using access control lists (ACLs) and on the fabric by using fabric binding.

- Access control lists (ACLs)
  - Include device connection and switch connection control policies
    - Device connection control policy specifies which HBAs, storage ports can be connected to a particular switch
    - Switch connection control policy prevents unauthorized switches to join a particular switch
- Fabric Binding
  - Prevents unauthorized switch from joining a fabric
- Role-based access control (RBAC)
  - Enables assigning roles to users that explicitly specify access rights

Logical Partitioning of a Fabric: Virtual SAN

- ➢ VSANs enable the creation of multiple logical SANs over a common physical SAN.
- ➢ They provide the capability to build larger consolidated fabrics and still maintain the required security and isolation between them.
- ➢ Fig 5.6 depicts logical partitioning in a VSAN.

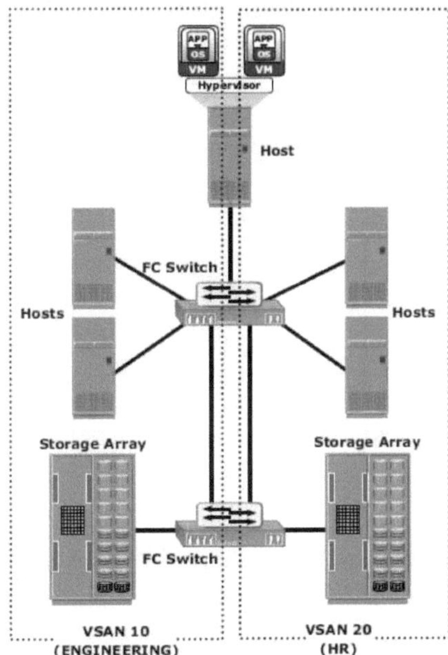

Fig 5.6: Securing SAN with VSAN

➤ The SAN administrator can create distinct VSANs by populating each of them with switch ports. In the example, the switch ports are distributed over two VSANs: 10 and 20 — for the Engineering and HR divisions, respectively. Although they share physical switching gear with other divisions, they can be managed individually as standalone fabrics. Zoning should be done for each VSAN to secure the entire physical SAN. Each managed VSAN can have only one active zone set at a time.

5.4.2 NAS

➤ NAS is open to multiple exploits, including viruses, worms, unauthorized access, snooping, and data tampering.

➤ Various security mechanisms are implemented in NAS to secure data and the storage networking infrastructure.

➤ Permissions and ACLs form the first level of protection to NAS resources by restricting accessibility and sharing. These permissions are deployed over and above the default behaviors and attributes associated with files and folders.

➤ In addition, various other authentication and authorization mechanisms, such as Kerberos and directory services, are implemented to verify the identity of network users and define their privileges. Similarly, firewalls protect the storage infrastructure from unauthorized access and malicious attacks.

NAS File Sharing: Windows ACLs

➤ Windows supports two types of ACLs:

    ○ discretionary access control lists (DACLs)

    ○ system access control lists (SACLs).

➤ The DACL, commonly referred to as the ACL, that determines access control. The SACL determines what accesses need to be audited if auditing is enabled.

➤ In addition to these ACLs, Windows also supports the concept of object ownership.

➤ The owner of an object has hard-coded rights to that object, and these rights do not need to be explicitly granted in the SACL.

➤ The owner, SACL, and DACL are all statically held as attributes of each object. Windows also offers the functionality to inherit permissions, which allows the child objects existing within a parent object to automatically inherit the ACLs of the parent object.

➤ ACLs are also applied to directory objects known as security identifiers (SIDs). These are automatically generated by a Windows server or domain when a user or group is created, and they are abstracted from the user.

> In this way, though a user may identify his login ID as "User1," it is simply a textual representation of the true SID, which is used by the underlying operating system.

> Internal processes in Windows refer to an account's SID rather than the account's username or group name while granting access to an object. ACLs are set by using the standard Windows Explorer GUI but can also be configured with CLI commands or other third-party tools.

NAS File Sharing: UNIX Permissions

> For the UNIX operating system, a user is an abstraction that denotes a logical entity for assignment of ownership and operation privileges for the system.

> A user can be either a person or a system operation.

> A UNIX system is only aware of the privileges of the user to perform specific operations on the system and identifies each user by a user ID (UID) and a username, regardless of whether it is a person, a system operation, or a device.

> In UNIX, users can be organized into one or more groups. The concept of group serves the purpose to assign sets of privileges for a given resource and sharing them among many users that need them.

> For example, a group of people working on one project may need the same permissions for a set of files.

> UNIX permissions specify the operations that can be performed by any ownership relation with respect to a file. These permissions specify what the owner can do, what the owner group can do, and what everyone else can do with the file.

> For any given ownership relation, three bits are used to specify access permissions. The first bit denotes read (r) access, the second bit denotes write (w) access, and the third bit denotes execute (x) access.

> Because UNIX defines three ownership relations (Owner, Group, and All), a triplet (defining the access permission) is required for each ownership relationship, resulting in nine bits. Each bit can be either set or clear. When displayed, a set bit is marked by its corresponding operation letter (r, w, or x), a clear bit is denoted by a dash (-), and all are put in a row, such as rwxr-xr-x. In this example, the owner can do anything with the file, but group owners and the rest of the world can read or execute only.

When displayed, a character denoting the mode of the file may precede this nine-bit pattern. For example, if the fi le is a directory, it is denoted as "d"; and if it is a link, it is denoted as "l."

NAS File Sharing: Authentication and Authorization

> In a file-sharing environment, NAS devices use standard file-sharing protocols, NFS and CIFS.

> Therefore, authentication and authorization are implemented and supported on NAS devices in the same way as in a UNIX or Windows file sharing environment.

> Authentication requires verifying the identity of a network user and therefore involves a login credential lookup on a Network Information System (NIS) server in a UNIX environment.Similarly, a Windows client is authenticated by a Windows domain controller that houses the Active Directory.

> The Active Directory uses LDAP to access information about network objects in the directory and Kerberos for network security. NAS devices use the same authentication techniques to validate network user credentials.

> Fig 5.7 depicts the authentication process in a NAS environment.

> Authorization defines user privileges in a network. The authorization techniques for UNIX users and Windows users are quite different. UNIX files use mode bits to define access rights granted to owners, groups, and other users, whereas Windows uses an ACL to allow or deny specific rights to a particular user for a particular file.

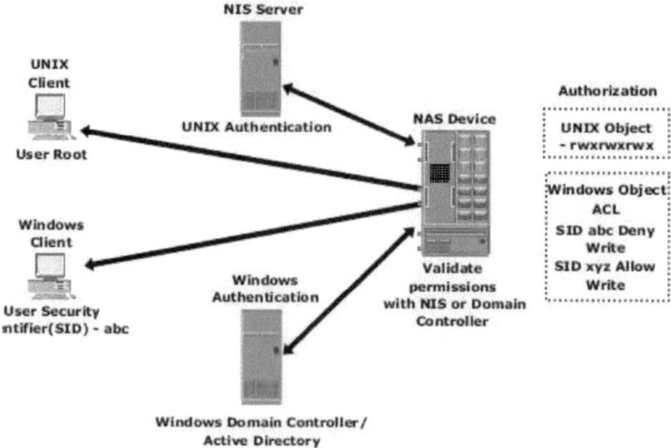

Fig 5.7 Securing user access in a NAS environment

Kerberos

> - Kerberos is a network authentication protocol, which is designed to provide strong authentication for client/server applications by using secret-key cryptography.
> - It uses cryptography so that a client and server can prove their identity to each other across an insecure network connection.
> - In Kerberos, authentications occur between clients and servers.
> - The client gets a ticket for a service and the server decrypts this ticket by using its secret key.
> - Any entity, user, or host that gets a service ticket for a Kerberos service is called a **Kerberos client.**
> - The term **Kerberos server** generally refers to the Key Distribution Center (KDC).
> - The KDC implements the Authentication Service (AS) and the Ticket Granting Service (TGS).
> - The KDC has a copy of every password associated with every principal, so it is absolutely vital that the KDC remain secure.
> - In Kerberos, users and servers for which a secret key is stored in the KDC database are known as *principals*.
> - In a NAS environment, Kerberos is primarily used when authenticating against a Microsoft Active Directory domain, although it can be used to execute security functions in UNIX environments.

The Kerberos authentication process shown in Fig 5.8 includes the following steps:

1. The user logs on to the workstation in the Active Directory domain (or forest) using an ID and a password. The client computer sends a request to the AS running on the KDC for a Kerberos ticket. The KDC verifies the user's login information from Active Directory.

2. The KDC responds with an encrypted Ticket Granting Ticket (TGT) and an encrypted session key. TGT has a limited validity period. TGT can be decrypted only by the KDC, and the client can decrypt only the session key.

3. When the client requests a service from a server, it sends a request, consisting of the previously generated TGT, encrypted with the sessionkey and the resource information to the

KDC.

4. The KDC checks the permissions in Active Directory and ensures that the user is authorized to use that service.

5. The KDC returns a service ticket to the client. This service ticket contains fields addressed to the client and to the server hosting the service.

6. The client then sends the service ticket to the server that houses the required resources.

7. The server, in this case the NAS device, decrypts the server portion of the ticket and stores the information in a key tab file. As long as the client's Kerberos ticket is valid, this authorization process does not need to be repeated. The server automatically allows the client to access the appropriate resources.

8. A client-server session is now established. The server returns a session ID to the client, which tracks the client activity, such as file locking, as long as the session is active.

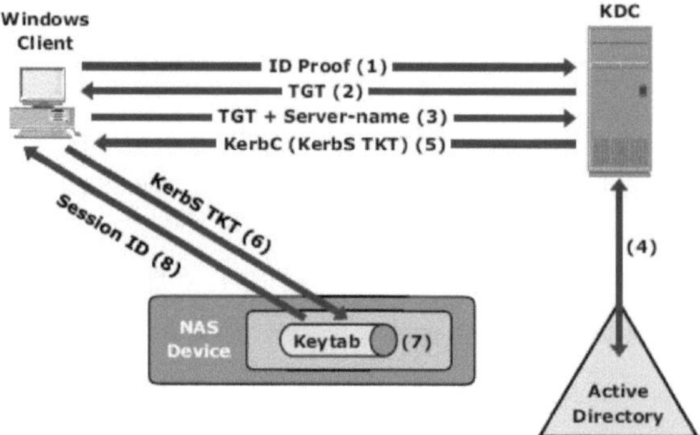

Fig 5.8 Kerberos authorization

Network-Layer Firewalls

- ➢ Because NAS devices utilize the IP protocol stack, they are vulnerable to various attacks initiated through the public IP network.
- ➢ Network layer firewalls are implemented in NAS environments to protect the NAS

devices from these security threats. These network-layer firewalls can examine network packets and compare them to a set of confi ed security rules. Packets that are not authorized by a security rule are dropped and not allowed to continue to the destination.

➤ Rules can be established based on a source address (network or host), a destination address (network or host), a port, or a combination of those factors (source IP, destination IP, and port number). The effectiveness of a firewall depends on how robust and extensive the security rules are.

➤ Fig 5.9 depicts a typical firewall implementation.

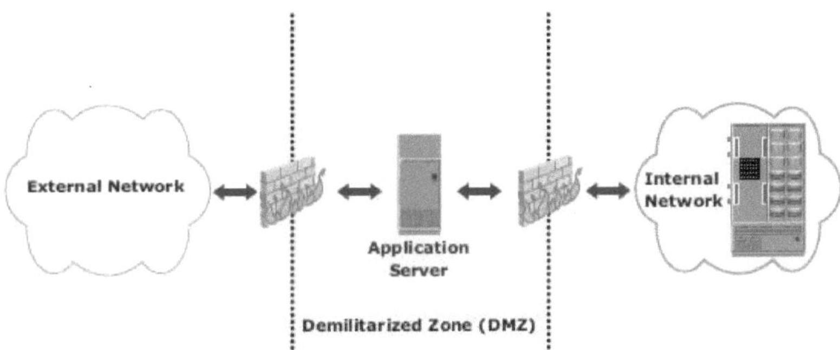

Fig 5.9: Securing a NAS environment with a network-layer firewall

➤ A demilitarized zone (DMZ) is commonly used in networking environments. A DMZ provides a means to secure internal assets while allowing Internet-based access to various resources. In a DMZ environment, servers that need to be accessed through the Internet are placed between two sets of firewalls.

➤ Application-specific ports, such as HTTP or FTP, are allowed through the firewall to the DMZ servers. No Internet-based traffic is allowed to penetrate the second set of firewalls and gain access to the internal network. The servers in the DMZ may or may not be allowed to communicate with internal resources.

➤ In such a setup, the server in the DMZ is an Internet-facing web application accessing data stored on a NAS device, which may be located on the internal private network. A secure design would serve only data to internal and external applications through the DMZ.

5.4.3 IP SAN

- The *Challenge-Handshake Authentication Protocol* (CHAP) is a basic authentication mechanism that has been widely adopted by network devices an hosts.
- CHAP provides a method for initiators and targets to authenticate each other by utilizing a secret code or password. CHAP secrets are usually random secrets of 12 to 128 characters.
- The secret is never exchanged directly over the communication channel; rather, a one-way hash function converts it into a hash value, which is then exchanged. A hash function, using the MD5 algorithm, transforms data in such a way that the result is unique and cannot be changed back to its original form. Fig 5.10 depicts the CHAP authentication process.

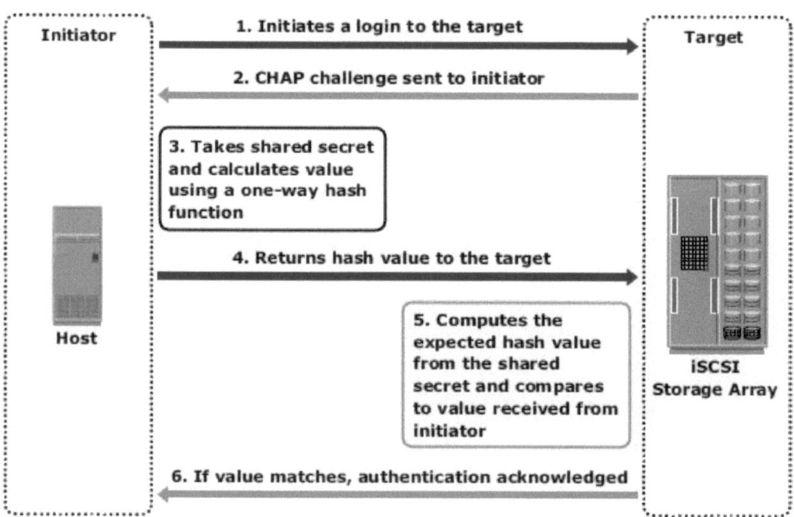

Fig 5.10 : Securing IPSAN with CHAP authentication

- If the initiator requires reverse CHAP authentication, the initiator authenticates the target by using the same procedure.
- The CHAP secret must be configured on the initiator and the target. A CHAP entry, composed of the name of a node and the secret associated with the node, is maintained by the target and the initiator.

➢ The same steps are executed in a two-way CHAP authentication scenario. After these steps are completed, the initiator authenticates the target. If both authentication steps succeed, then data access is allowed.

➢ CHAP is often used because it is a fairly simple protocol to implement and can be implemented across a number of disparate systems.

➢ *iSNS discovery domains* function in the same way as FC zones. Discovery domains provide functional groupings of devices in an IP-SAN.

➢ For devices to communicate with one another, they must be confi gured in the same discovery domain.

➢ State change notifications (SCNs) inform the iSNS server when devices are added to or removed from a discovery domain. Fig 5.11 depicts the discovery domains in iSNS.

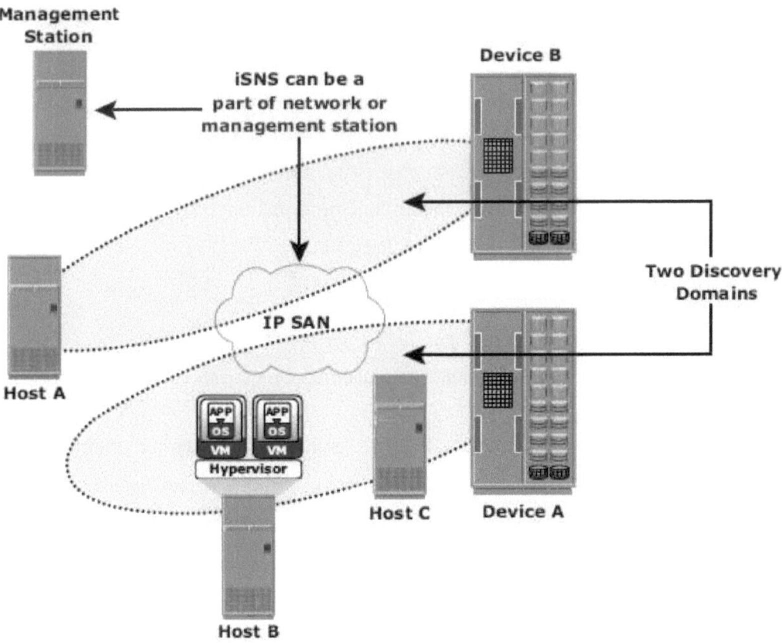

Fig 5.11 : Securing IPSAN with iSNS discovery domains

5.5 Securing Storage Infrastructure in Virtualizedand Cloud Environments

5.5.1 Security Concerns

> Organizations are rapidly adopting virtualization and cloud computing, however they have some security concerns.

> The key security concerns are multitenancy, velocity of attack, information assurance, and data privacy.

> **Multitenancy**, by virtue of virtualization, enables multiple independent tenants to be serviced using the same set of storage resources.

> **Velocity-of-attack** refers to a situation in which any existing security threat in the cloud spreads more rapidly and has a larger impact than that in the traditional data center environments.

> **Information assurance** for users ensures confidentiality, integrity, and availability of data in the cloud.

> Also the cloud user needs assurance that all the users operating on the cloud are genuine and access the data only with legitimate rights and scope.

> Data privacy is also a major concern in a virtualized and cloud environment. A CSP needs to ensure that Personally Identifiable Information (PII) about its clients is legally protected from any unauthorized disclosure.

5.5.2 Security Measures

> Security measures can be implemented at the compute, network, and storage levels.

Security at the Compute Level

> Securing a compute infrastructure includes enforcing the security of the physical server, hypervisor, VM, and guest OS (OS running within a virtual machine).

> Physical server security involves implementing user authentication and authorization mechanisms. These mechanisms identify users and provide access privileges on the server.

> To minimize the attack surface on the server, unused hardware components, such as NICs, USB ports, or drives, should be removed or disabled.

> A hypervisor is a single point of security failure for all the VMs running on it. Rootkits and malware installed on a hypervisor make detection difficult for the antivirus software installed on the guest OS. To protect against attacks, security-

critical hypervisor updates should be installed regularly.

➢ The hypervisor management system must also be protected.

➢ VM isolation and hardening are some of the common security mechanisms to effectively safeguard a VM from an attack. VM isolation helps to prevent a compromised guest OS from impacting other guest OSs. VM isolation is implemented at the hypervisor level.

➢ Hardening is a process to change the default configuration to achieve greater security.

➢ Apart from the measures to secure a hypervisor and VMs, virtualized andncloud environments also require further measures on the guest OS and application levels.

Security at the Network Level

➢ The key security measures that minimize vulnerabilities at the network layer are firewall, intrusion detection, demilitarized zone (DMZ), and encryption of data-in-flight.

➢ A firewall protects networks from unauthorized access while permitting only legitimate communications. In a virtualized and cloud environment, a firewall can also protect hypervisors and VMs.

➢ Intrusion Detection (ID) is the process to detect events that can compromise the confidentiality, integrity, or availability of a resource.

Security at the Storage Level

➢ Major threats to storage systems in virtualized and cloud environments arise due to compromises at compute, network, and physical security levels. This is because access to storage systems is through compute and network infrastructure. Therefore, adequate security measures should be in place at the compute and network levels to ensure storage security.

➢ Common security mechanisms that protect storage include the following:

  o Access control methods to regulate which users and processes access the data on the storage systems

  o Zoning and LUN masking

  o Encryption of data-at-rest (on the storage system) and data-in-transit. Data encryption should also include encrypting backups and storing encryption keys separately from the data.

  o Data shredding that removes the traces of the deleted data

5.6 Monitoring the Storage Infrastructure

- ➢ Monitoring is one of the most important aspects that forms the basis for managing storage infrastructure resources. Monitoring provides the performance and accessibility status of various components. Monitoring also helps to analyze the utilization and consumption of various storage infrastructure resources.

5.6.1 Monitoring Parameters

- ➢ Storage infrastructure components should be monitored for accessibility, capacity, performance, and security.
- ➢ **Accessibility** refers to the availability of a component to perform its desired operation during a specified time period.
- ➢ **Capacity** refers to the amount of storage infrastructure resources available.
- ➢ **Performance** monitoring evaluates how efficiently different storage infrastructure components are performing and helps to identify bottlenecks.
- ➢ **Security** monitoring helps to track unauthorized configuration changes to storage infrastructure resources.

5.6.2 Components Monitored

- ➢ The components within the storage environment that should be monitored are:
  - o Hosts,
  - o networks, and
  - o storage
- ➢ The components are monitored for below parameters:
  - o accessibility,
  - o capacity,
  - o performance, and
  - o security.
- ➢ These components can be physical or virtualized.

Hosts:

- ➢ **The accessibility** of a host depends on the availability status of the hardware components and the software processes running on it.
- ➢ For example, a host's NIC (hardware) failure might cause inaccessibility of the host to its user.

- Server clustering is a mechanism that provides high availability if a server failure occurs.
- ***Capacity monitoring of the file system utilization*** is important to ensure that sufficient capacity is available to the applications, otherwise this disrupts application availability.
- Administrator can extend (manually or automatically) the file system's space proactively to prevent application outage.
- Use of virtual provisioning technology enables efficient management of storage capacity requirements but is highly dependent on capacity monitoring.
- ***Performance monitoring of the host*** mainly involves a status check on the utilization of various server resources, such as *CPU* and *memory*.
- High utilization leads to *degraded performance and slower response time*.
- Actions taken by administrators to correct the problem are, *upgrading or adding more processors and shifting the workload to different servers*.
- In a virtualized environment, *additional CPU and memory* may be allocated to VMs dynamically from the pool, if available, to meet performance requirements.
- ***Security monitoring*** on servers involves tracking of login failures and execution of unauthorized applications or software processes.
- Proactive measures against unauthorized access to the servers are based on the threat identified.
- For example, an administrator can block user access if multiple login failures are logged.

Storage Network

- **Storage networks** need to be monitored to ensure uninterrupted communication between the server and the storage array.
- **Accessibility:** Uninterrupted access to data depends on the accessibility of both the physical and logical components.
- The physical components include **switches, ports, and cables**.
- The logical components include constructs, such as **zones**.
- Any failure in the physical or logical components causes **data unavailability**.
- **Capacity monitoring** in a storage network involves monitoring the number of available ports in the fabric, the utilization of the interswitch links, or individual ports,

and each interconnect device in the fabric.

- ➤ **Performance monitoring** of the storage network enables assessing individual component performance and helps to identify network bottlenecks.
- ➤ For IP networks, monitoring the performance includes monitoring network latency, packet loss, bandwidth utilization for I/O, network errors, packet retransmission rates, and collisions.
- ➤ **Security monitoring** of storage network provides information about any unauthorized change to the configuration of the fabric.
- ➤ Login failures and unauthorized access to switches for performing administrative changes should be logged and monitored continuously.

Storage

- ➤ **The accessibility** of the storage array should be monitored for its hardware components and various processes.
- ➤ Storage arrays are configured with redundant hardware components, and therefore individual component failure does not affect their accessibility.
- ➤ Failure of any process in the storage array might disrupt or compromise business operations. Example: failure of a replication task affects disaster recovery capabilities.
- ➤ Some storage arrays provide the capability to send messages to the vendor's support center if hardware or process failures occur, referred to as a call home.
- ➤ **Capacity monitoring** of a storage array enables the administrator to respond to storage needs preemptively based on capacity utilization and consumption trends.
- ➤ Information about unconfigured and unallocated storage space enables the administrator to decide whether a new server can be allocated storage capacity from the storage array.
- ➤ **Performance monitoring** of a storage array involves using a number of performance metrics, such as utilization rates of the various storage array components, I/O response time, and cache utilization.
- ➤ A storage array is usually a shared resource, which may be exposed to security threats. **Monitoring security** helps to track unauthorized configuration of the storage array and ensures that only authorized users are allowed to access it.

5.6.3 Monitoring Examples

Accessibility Monitoring

- Failure of any component might affect the accessibility of one or more components due to their interconnections and dependencies.
- Consider an implementation in a storage infrastructure with three servers: H1, H2, and H3. All the servers are configured with two HBAs, each connected to the production storage array through two switches, SW1 and SW2, as shown in Fig 5.12.
- All the servers share two storage ports on the storage array and multipathing software is installed on all the servers.
- If one of the switches (SW1) fails, the multipathing software initiates a path failover, and all the servers continue to access data through the other switch, SW2.
- Due to the absence of a redundant switch, a second switch failure could result in inaccessibility of the array.
- Monitoring for accessibility enables detecting the switch failure and helps an administrator to take corrective action before another failure occurs.
- In most cases, the administrator receives symptom alerts for a failing component and can initiate actions before the component fails.

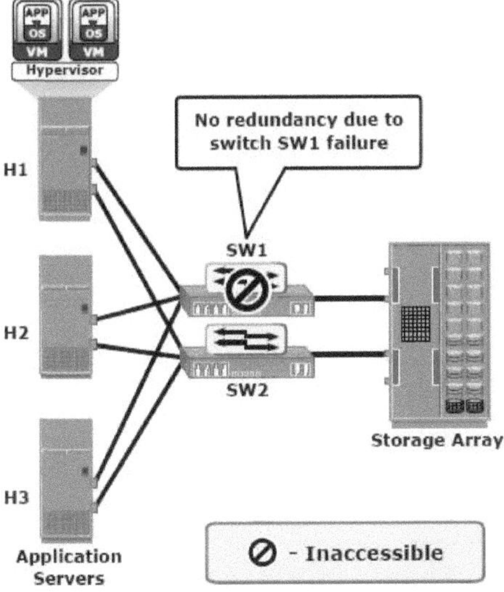

Fig 5.12: Switch failure in a storage infrastructure

Capacity Monitoring

> In the scenario shown in Fig 5.13, servers H1, H2, and H3 are connected to the production array through two switches, SW1 and SW2. Each of the servers is allocated storage on the storage array.

> When a new server is deployed in this configuration, the applications on the new server need to be given storage capacity from the production storage array.

> Monitoring the available capacity on the array helps to decide whether the array can provide the required storage to the new server.

> Also, monitoring the available number of ports on SW1 and SW2 helps to   decide whether the new server can be connected to the switches.

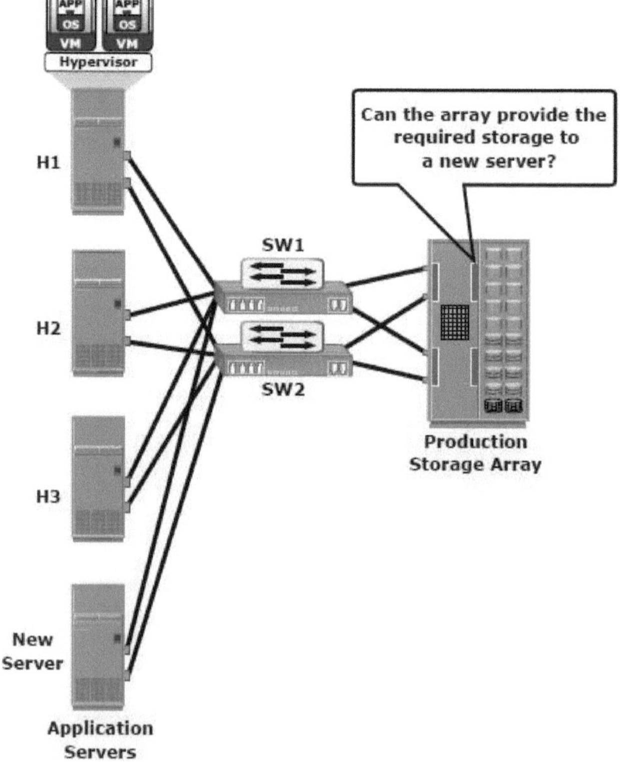

Fig 5.13: Monitoring storage array capacity

➤ The following example illustrates the importance of monitoring the file system capacity on file servers. Fig 5.14 (a) illustrates the environment of a file system when full and that results in application outage when no capacity monitoring is implemented.

➤ Monitoring can be configured to issue a message when thresholds are reached on the file system capacity. For example, when the file system reaches 66 percent of its capacity, a warning message is issued, and a critical message is issued when the file system reaches 80 percent of its capacity (Fig 5.14 [b]). This enables the administrator to take action to extend the file system before it runs out of capacity. Proactively monitoring the file system can prevent application outages caused due to lack of file system space.

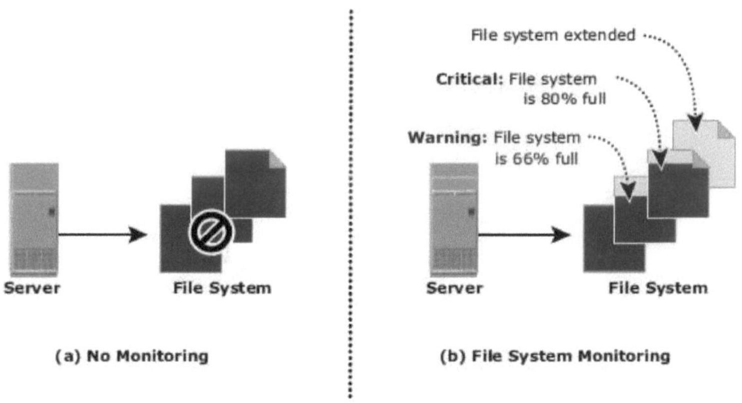

Fig 5.14: Monitoring server file system space

Performance Monitoring

➤ The example shown in Fig 5.15 illustrates the importance of monitoring performance on storage arrays.

➤ In this example, servers H1, H2, and H3 (with two HBAs each) are connected to the storage array through switch SW1 and SW2. The three servers share the same storage ports on the storage array to access LUNs.

➤ A new server running an application with a high work load must be deployed to share the same storage port as H1, H2, and H3.

➤ Monitoring array port utilization ensures that the new server does not adversely affect the performance of the other servers.

- ➤ In this example, utilization of the shared storage port is shown by the solid and dotted lines in the graph.
- ➤ If the port utilization prior to deploying the new server is close to 100 percent, then deploying the new server is not recommended because it might impact the performance of the other servers. However, if the utilization of the port prior to deploying the new server is closer to the dotted line, then there is room to add a new server.

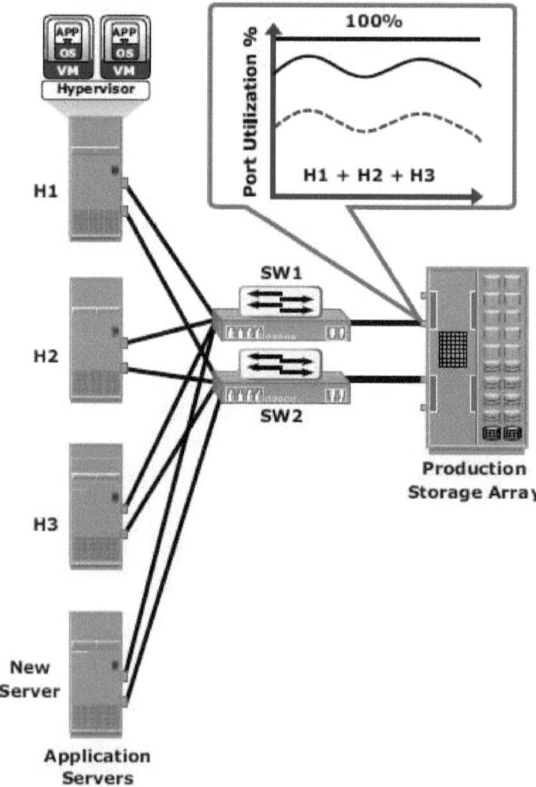

Fig 5.15: Monitoring array port utilization

Security Monitoring

- ➢ The example shown in Fig 5.16 illustrates the importance of monitoring security in a storage array.
- ➢ In this example, the storage array is shared between two workgroups, WG1 and WG2. The data of WG1 should not be accessible to WG2 and vice versa. A user from WG1 might try to make a local replica of the data that belongs to WG2.
- ➢ If this action is not monitored or recorded, it is difficult to track such a violation of information security. If this action is monitored, a warning message can be sent to prompt a corrective action or at least enable discovery as part of regular auditing operations.
- ➢ An example of host security monitoring is tracking of login attempts at the host. The login is authorized if the login ID and password entered are correct; or the login attempt fails. These login failures might be accidental (mistyping) or a deliberate attempt to access a server. Many servers usually allow a fixed number of successive login failures, prohibiting any additional attempts after these login failures.
- ➢ In a monitored environment, the login information is recorded in a system log file, and three successive login failures trigger a message, warning of a possible security threat.

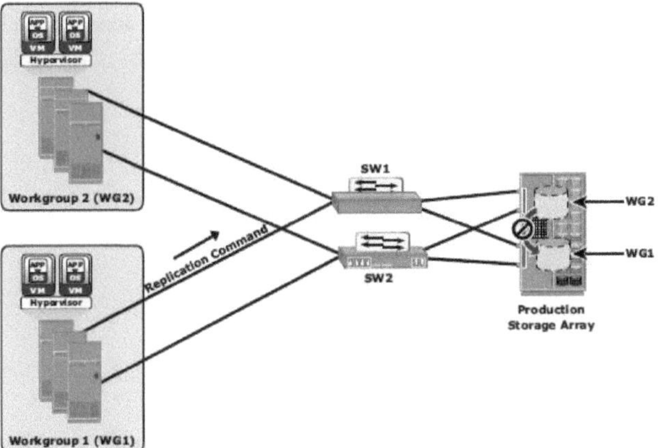

Fig 5.16: Monitoring security in a storage array

5.6.4 Alerts

➢ Alerting of events is an integral part of monitoring. Alerting keeps administrators informed about the status of various components and processes — for example, conditions such as failure of power, disks, memory, or switches, which can impact the availability of services and require immediate administrative attention. Other conditions, such as a file system reaching a capacity threshold are considered warning signs and may also require administrative attention.

➢ Monitoring tools enable administrators to assign different severity levels based on the impact of the alerted condition.

➢ Whenever a condition with a particular severity level occurs, an alert is sent to the administrator, a script is triggered, or an incident ticket is opened to initiate a corrective action.

➢ Alert classifications can range from information alerts to fatal alerts.

➢ **Information alerts** provide useful information but do not require any intervention by the administrator.

➢ **Warning alerts** require administrative attention so that the alerted condition is contained and does not affect accessibility.

➢ **Fatal alerts** require immediate attention because the condition might affect overall performance, security, or availability.

➢ Continuous monitoring, with automated alerting, enables administrators to respond to failures quickly and proactively. Alerting provides information that helps administrators prioritize their response to events.

5.7 Storage Infrastructure Management Activities

➢ The key storage infrastructure management activities performed in a data center can be broadly categorized into:

  o availability management,
  o capacity management,
  o performance management,
  o security management, and
  o reporting.

5.7.1 Availability Management

➢ Availability management requires establishing a proper guideline based on defined **service levels** to ensure availability.

➢ *Availability management* involves all availability-related issues for components or services to ensure that service levels are met.

➢ In availability management, the key activity is to provision **redundancy** at all levels, including components, data, or even sites.

➢ Eg: When a server is deployed to support critical business function, it requires high availability by deploying two or more HBAs, multipathing software, and server clustering.

➢ The server must be connected to the storage array using at least two independent fabrics and switches that have built-in redundancy.

➢ In addition, the storage arrays should have built-in redundancy for various components and should support local and remote replication.

5.7.2 Capacity Management

➢ The goal of **capacity management** is to ensure adequate *availability* of resources based on their service level requirements.

➢ Capacity management also involves *optimization* of capacity based on the cost and future needs.

➢ Capacity management provides *capacity analysis* that compares allocated storage to forecasted storage on a regular basis.

➢ It also provides *trend analysis* based on the rate of consumption, which must be rationalized against storage acquisition and deployment timetables.

➢ **Storage provisioning** is an example of capacity management which involves activities, such as creating RAID sets and LUNs, and allocating them to the host.

➢ **Enforcing capacity quotas** for users is another example of capacity management. Provisioning a fixed amount of user quotas restricts users from exceeding the allocated capacity.

➢ *Data deduplication and compression*, have reduced the amount of data to be backed up and thereby reduced the amount of storage capacity to be managed.

5.7.3 Performance Management

- **Performance management** ensures the optimal operational efficiency of all components.

- Performance analysis helps to identify the performance of storage infrastructure components and provides information on whether a component meets expected performance levels.

- Several performance management activities need to be performed when deploying a new application or server in the existing storage infrastructure.

- For example, to optimize the expected performance levels, *fine-tuning* is required for activities on the server, such as the volume configuration, database design or application layout, configuration of multiple HBAs, and intelligent multipathing software.

- The performance management tasks on a SAN include designing and implementing *sufficient ISLs* in a multiswitch fabric with adequate bandwidth to support the required performance levels.

- The storage array configuration tasks include selecting the appropriate RAID type, LUN layout, front-end ports, back-end ports, and cache configuration, when considering the end-to-end performance.

5.7.4 Security Management

- The key objective of the *security management* activity is to ensure **confidentiality**, **integrity**, and **availability** of information in both virtualized and nonvirtualized environments.

- Security management *prevents unauthorized* access and configuration of storage infrastructure components.

- For example, while deploying an application or a server, the security management tasks include *managing the user accounts and access policies* that authorize users to perform role-based activities.

- The security management tasks in a SAN environment include configuration of zoning to restrict an unauthorized HBA from accessing specific storage array ports.

- The security management task on a storage array includes LUN masking that restricts a host's access to intended LUNs only.

5.7.5 Reporting

- **Reporting** on a storage infrastructure involves keeping track and gathering information from various components and processes.
- This information is compiled to generate reports for **trend analysis, capacity planning, chargeback,** and **performance**.
- *Capacity planning reports* contain current and historic information about the utilization of storage, file systems, database tablespace, ports, and so on.
- *Configuration and asset management reports* include details about device allocation, local or remote replicas, and fabric configuration. It also lists all the equipment, with details of their purchase date, lease status, and maintenance records.
- *Chargeback reports* contain information about the allocation or utilization of storage infrastructure components by various departments or user groups.
- *Performance reports* provide details about the performance of various storage infrastructure components.

5.7.6 Storage Infrastructure Management in a Virtualized Environment

- Storage virtualization has enabled dynamic migration of data and extension of storage volumes. Due to dynamic extension, storage volumes can be expanded nondisruptively to meet both capacity and performance requirements.
- Since virtualization breaks the bond between the storage volumes presented to the host and its physical storage, data can be migrated both within and across data centers without any downtime. This has made the administrator's tasks *easier* while reconfiguring the physical environment.
- ***Virtual storage provisioning*** is another tool that has changed the infrastructure management cost and complexity scenario.
- In conventional provisioning, storage capacity is provisioned upfront in anticipation of future growth. This results in overutilization or underutilization issues.
- Use of virtual provisioning can address this challenge and make capacity management less challenging. In virtual provisioning, storage is allocated from the shared pool to hosts on-demand. This improves the storage capacity utilization, and thereby reduces capacity management complexities.
- Virtualization has also contributed to network management efficiency. VSANs and VLANs made the administrator's job easier by isolating different networks logically

using management tools rather than physically separating them.

➤ Disparate virtual networks can be created on a single physical network, and reconfiguration of nodes can be done quickly without any physical changes.

➤ It has also addressed some of the security issues that might exist in a conventional environment.

➤ On the host side, compute virtualization has made host deployment, reconfiguration, and migration easier than physical environment.

➤ Compute, application, and memory virtualization have not only improved provisioning, but also contributed to the high availability of resources.

STORAGE MULTITENANCY

➤ Multiple tenants sharing the same resources provided by a single landlord (resource provider) is called **multitenancy**.

➤ Two common examples of multitenancy are:
  o multiple virtual machines sharing the same server hardware through the use of a hypervisor running on the server,
  o multiple user applications using the same storage platform.

➤ **Security** and **service level assurance** are a key concerns in any multitenant storage environment.

➤ *Secure multitenancy* means that no tenant can access another tenant's data.

➤ Below are the four pillars of multitenancy:
  o **Secure separation:** This enables data path separation across various tenants in a multitenant environment. This pillar can be divided into four basic requirements: separation of data at rest, address space separation, authentication and name service separation, and separation of data access.

  o **Service assurance:** Consistent and reliable service levels are integral to storage multitenancy. Service assurance plays an important role in providing service levels that can be unique to each tenant.

  o **Availability:** High availability ensures a resilient architecture that provides fault tolerance and redundancy. This is even more critical when storage infrastructure is shared by multiple tenants, because the impact of any outage is magnified.

o **Management:** This includes provisions that allow a landlord to manage basic infrastructure while delegating management responsibilities to tenants for the resources that they interact with day to day. This concept is known as balancing the provider (landlord) in-control with the tenant in-control capabilities.

5.7.7 Storage Management Examples

Example 1: Storage Allocation to a New Server/Host
➤ Consider the deployment of a new RDBMS server to the existing **nonvirtualized storage infrastructure environment**.

➤ Below are the storage management activities, performed by the administrator:
1. Install and configure the HBAs and device drivers on the server before it is physically connected to the SAN. Multipathing software can also be installed on the server.
2. Connect storage array ports to the SAN and perform zoning on the SAN switches to allow the new server access to the storage array ports via its HBAs.
3. Ensure redundant paths between the server and the storage array by connecting the HBAs of the new server to different switches and zoning with different array ports.
4. Configure LUNs on the array and assign these LUNs to the storage array front-end ports. LUN masking configuration is performed on the storage array, which restricts access to LUNs by a specific server.
5. The server then discovers the LUNs assigned to it by either a bus rescan process or sometimes through a server reboot, depending upon the operating system installed.
6. A volume manager may be used to configure the logical volumes and file systems on the host. The number of logical volumes or file systems to be created depends on how a database or an application is expected to use the storage.
7. Install database or an application on the logical volumes or file systems that were created.
8. The last step is to make the database or application capable of using the new file system space.

➤ Fig 5.17 illustrates the activities performed on a server, a SAN, and a storage array for the allocation of storage to a new server.

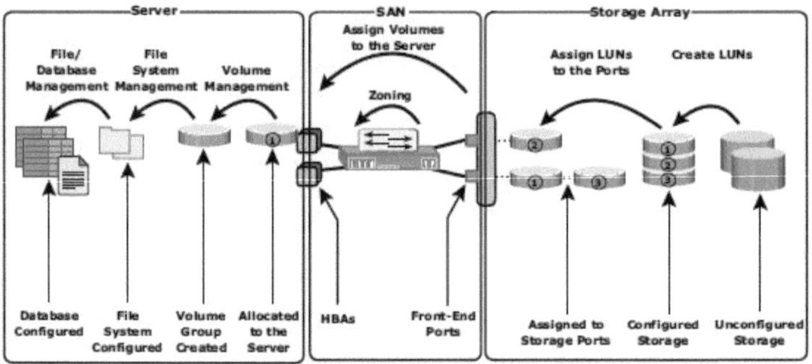

Fig 5.17: Storage allocation tasks

➤ Below are the various administrative tasks performed in a **virtualized environment** to provision storage to a VM that runs an RDBMS.

1. Similar to nonvirtualized environment, a physical connection must be established between the physical server, which hosts the VMs, and the storage array through the SAN.

2. At the SAN level, a VSAN can be configured to transfer data between the physical server and the storage array. This isolates storage traffic from any other traffic in the SAN. Zoning can be configured within the VSAN.

3. At the storage side, administrators need to create thin LUNs from the shared storage pool and assign these thin LUNs to the storage array front-end ports. LUN masking needs to be carried out on the storage array.

4. At the physical server side, the hypervisor discovers the assigned LUNs. The hypervisor creates a logical volume and file system to store and manage VM files.

5. Administrator creates a VM and installs the OS and RDBMS on the VM. During this, the hypervisor creates a virtual disk file and other VM files in the hypervisor file system. The virtual disk file appears to the VM as a SCSI disk and is used to store the RDBMS data. Alternatively, the hypervisor enables virtual provisioning to create a thin virtual disk and assigns it to the VM.

6. Hypervisors usually have native multipathing capabilities. Optionally, a third-party multipathing software may be installed on the hypervisor.

Example 2: File System Space Management

> To prevent a file system from running out of space, administrators need to perform tasks to offload data from the existing file system.

> This includes deleting unwanted files or archiving data that is not accessed for a long time.

> Alternatively, an administrator can *extend the file system* to increase its size and avoid an application outage.

> The dynamic extension of file systems or a logical volume depends on the operating system or the logical volume manager (LVM) in use.

> Fig 5.18 shows the steps and considerations for the extension of file systems in the flow chart.

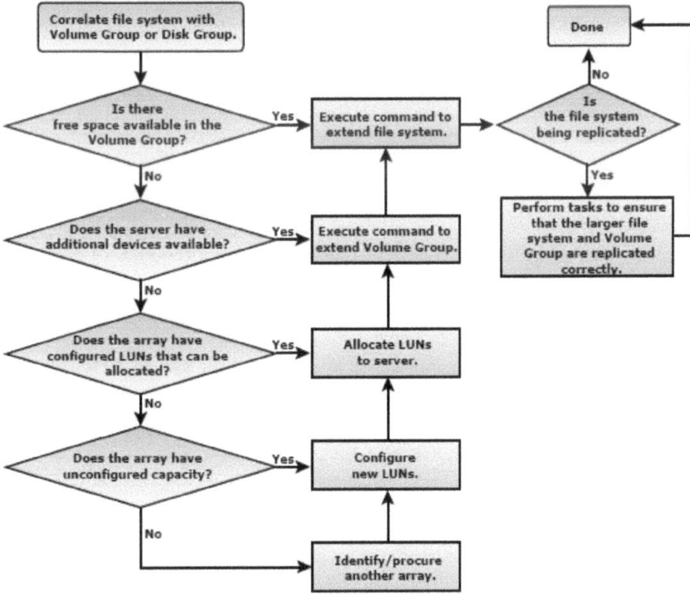

Fig 5.18: Extending a file system

Example 3: Chargeback Report

> This example explores the storage infrastructure management tasks necessary to create a **chargeback report**.

> Fig 5.19 shows a configuration deployed in a storage infrastructure. Three servers with two HBAs each connect to a storage array via two switches, SW1 and SW2.

> Array replication technology is used to create local and remote replicas. The production device is represented as A, the local replica device as B, and the remote replica device as C.

> Individual departmental applications run on each of the servers.

> A report documenting the exact amount of storage resources used by each application is created using a *chargeback analysis* for each department.

> If the unit for billing is based on the amount of *raw storage* (usable capacity plus protection provided) configured for an application used by a department, the exact amount of raw space configured must be reported for each application.

> Fig 5.19 shows a sample report for two applications, *Payroll_1* and *Engineering_1*.

> The first step to determine chargeback costs is to correlate the application with the exact amount of raw storage configured for that application.

> Fig 5.20 shows the storage space used for Payroll_1 application identified based on file systems to logical volumes to volume groups and to the LUNs on the array.

> When the applications are replicated, the storage space used for local replication and remote replication is also identified.

> In the example shown, Payroll_1 is using *Source Vol 1* and *Vol 2* (in the production array). The replication volumes are *Local Replica Vol 1* and *Vol 2* (in the production array) and *Remote Replica Vol 1* and *Vol 2* (in the remote array).

> Based on this example, consider that Source Vol 1 and Vol 2 are each 50 GB in size, the storage allocated to the application is 100 GB (50 + 50). The **allocated storage** for replication is 100 GB for local replication and 100 GB for remote replication.

> The **raw storage** configured for the application is determined from the allocated storage based on the RAID protection that is used.

> If the Payroll_1 application's production volumes are RAID 1-protected, the raw space used is 200 GB.

> Assume the local replicas are on unprotected volumes, and the remote replicas are protected with a RAID 5 configuration, then 100 GB of raw space is used by the local

replica and 125 GB by the remote replica.

- ➢ Therefore, the total raw capacity used by the Payroll_1 application is 425 GB. The total cost of storage provisioned for Payroll_1 application will be $2,125 (assume cost per GB of storage is $5).

- ➢ This exercise must be repeated for each application in the enterprise (eg: Engineering_1, etc) to generate the chargeback report.

- ➢ Chargeback reports can be extended to include a pre-established cost of other resources, such as the number of switch ports, HBAs, and array ports in the configuration.

- ➢ Chargeback reports are used by data center administrators to ensure that storage consumers are well aware of the costs of the services that they have requested.

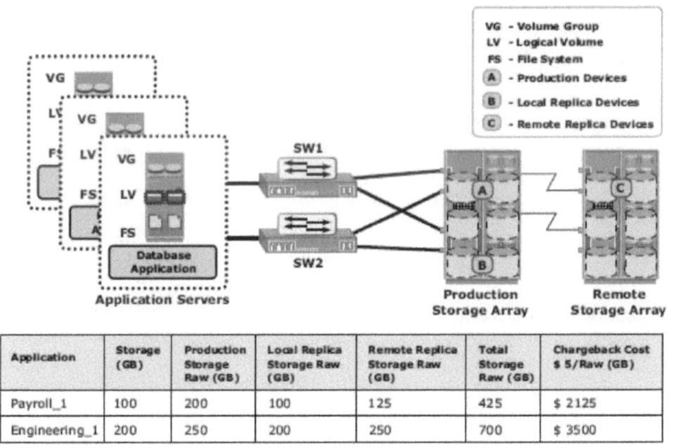

Application	Storage (GB)	Production Storage Raw (GB)	Local Replica Storage Raw (GB)	Remote Replica Storage Raw (GB)	Total Storage Raw (GB)	Chargeback Cost $ 5/Raw (GB)
Payroll_1	100	200	100	125	425	$ 2125
Engineering_1	200	250	200	250	700	$ 3500

Fig 5.19: Configuration and Chargeback report

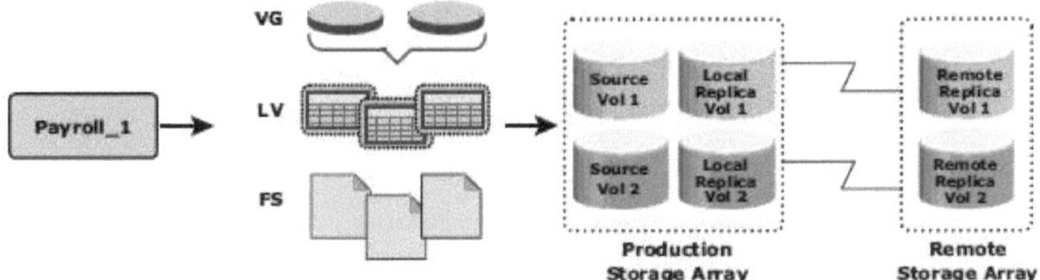

Fig 5.20: Correlation of capacity configured for an application

5.8 Storage Infrastructure Management Challenges

- The main challenge in monitoring and managing today's complex storage infrastructure is due to the heterogeneity of storage arrays, networks, servers, databases, and applications in the environment.
- Eg: heterogeneous storage arrays vary in their capacity, performance, protection, and architectures. Each of the components in a data center typically comes with vendor-specific tools for management.
- An environment with multiple tools makes understanding the overall status of the environment challenging because the tools may not be interoperable.
- Ideally, management tools should correlate information from all components in one place. Such tools provide an end-to-end view of the environment, and a quicker root cause analysis for faster resolution to alerts.

5.9 Information Lifecycle Management

- In both traditional data center and virtualized environments, managing information can be expensive if not managed appropriately.
- Along with the tools, an effective management strategy is also required to manage information efficiently.
- This strategy should address the following key challenges that exist in today's data centers:
    - **Exploding digital universe:** The rate of information growth is increasing exponentially. Creating copies of data to ensure high availability and repurposing has contributed to the multifold increase of information growth.
    - **Increasing dependency on information:** The strategic use of information plays an important role in determining the success of a business and provides competitive advantages in the marketplace.
    - **Changing value of information:** Information that is valuable today might become less important tomorrow. The value of information often changes over time.
- Framing a strategy to meet these challenges involves understanding the value of information over its life cycle.
- When information is first created, it often has the highest value and is accessed

frequently. As the information ages, it is accessed less frequently and is of less value to the organization. Understanding the value of information helps to deploy the appropriate infrastructure according to the changing value of information.

➢ For example, in a sales order application, the value of the information (customer data) changes from the time the order is placed until the time that the warranty becomes void (see Fig 5.21).

➢ The value of the information is highest when a company receives a new sales order and processes it to deliver the product. After the order fulfillment, the customer data does not need to be available for real-time access.

➢ The company can transfer this data to less expensive secondary storage with lower performance until a warranty claim or another event triggers its need.

➢ After the warranty becomes void, the company can dispose of the information.

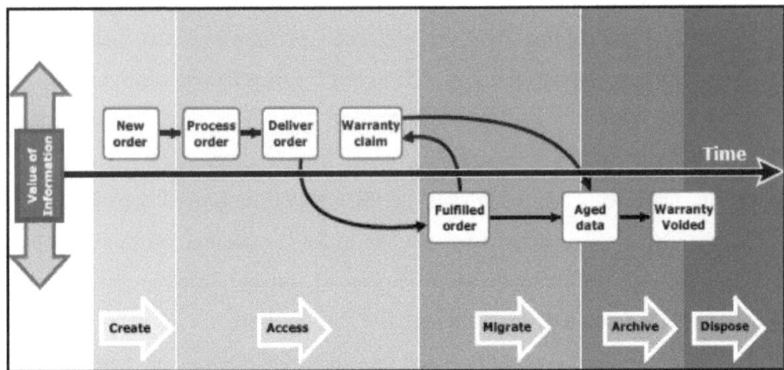

Fig 5.21 Changing value of sales order information

➢ **Information Lifecycle Management (ILM)** is a proactive strategy that enables an IT organization to effectively manage information throughout its life cycle based on predefined business policies.

➢ From data creation to data deletion, ILM aligns the business requirements and processes with service levels in an automated fashion. This allows an IT organization to optimize the storage infrastructure for maximum return on investment.

➢ Implementing an ILM strategy has the following key benefits that directly address the challenges of information management:

  o **Lower Total Cost of Ownership (TCO):** By aligning the infrastructure and management costs with information value. As a result, resources are not wasted, and complexity is not introduced by managing low-value data at the expense of high-value data.

- o **Simplified management:** By integrating process steps and interfaces with individual tools and by increasing automation
- o **Maintaining compliance**: By knowing what data needs to be protected for what length of time
- o **Optimized utilization**: By deploying storage tiering

5.10 Storage Tiering

- ➢ Storage tiering is a technique of establishing a hierarchy of different storage types (tiers). This enables storing the right data to the right tier, based on service level requirements, at a minimal cost.
- ➢ Each tier has different levels of protection, performance, and cost. For example, high performance solidstate drives (SSDs) or FC drives can be configured as tier 1 storage to keep frequently accessed data, and low cost SATA drives as tier 2 storage to keep the less frequently accessed data.
- ➢ Keeping frequently used data in SSD or FC improves application performance. Moving less-frequently accessed data to SATA can free up storage capacity in high performance drives and reduce the cost of storage. This movement of data happens based on defined tiering policies.
- ➢ The tiering policy might be based on parameters, such as file type, size, frequency of access, and so on. For example, if a policy states "Move the files that are not accessed for the last 30 days to the lower tier," then all the files matching this condition are moved to the lower tier.
- ➢ Storage tiering can be implemented as **a manual or an automated process.**
- ➢ Manual storage tiering is the traditional method where the storage administrator monitors the storage workloads periodically and moves the data between the tiers. Manual storage tiering is complex and time-consuming.
- ➢ Automated storage tiering automates the storage tiering process, in which data movement between the tiers is performed nondisruptively. In automated storage tiering, the application workload is proactively monitored; the active data is automatically moved to a higher performance tier and the inactive data to a higher

capacity, lower performance tier.

➢ Data movements between various tiers can happen within (**intra-array**) or between (**inter-array**) storage arrays.

5.10.1 Intra-Array Storage Tiering

➢ The process of storage tiering within a storage array is called intra-array storage tiering.

➢ It enables the efficient use of SSD, FC, and SATA drives within an array and provides performance and cost optimization.

➢ The goal is to keep the SSDs busy by storing the most frequently accessed data on them, while moving out the less frequently accessed data to the SATA drives.

➢ Data movements executed between tiers can be performed at the LUN level or at the sub-LUN level.

➢ The performance can be further improved by implementing tiered cache.

➢ **LUN tiering, sub-LUN tiering,** and **cache tiering** are explained next.

➢ Traditionally, storage tiering is operated at the LUN level that moves an entire LUN from one tier of storage to another (see Fig 5.22 [a]).

➢ This movement includes both active and inactive data in that LUN.

➢ This method does not give effective cost and performance benefits.

➢ Today, storage tiering can be implemented at the sub-LUN level (see Fig 5.22 [b]).

➢ In sub-LUN level tiering, a LUN is broken down into smaller segments and tiered at that level. Movement of data with much finer granularity, for example 8 MB, greatly enhances the value proposition of automated storage tiering.

➢ Tiering at the sub-LUN level effectively moves active data to faster drives and less active data to slower drives.

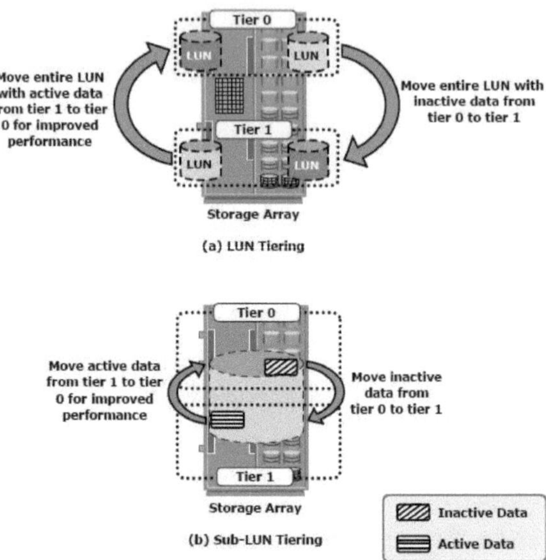

Fig 5.22: Implementation of intra-array storage tiering

15.10.2 Inter-Array Storage Tiering

- ➢ The process of storage tiering between storage arrays is called inter-array storage tiering. Inter-array storage tiering automates the identification of active or inactive data to relocate them to different performance or capacity tiers between the arrays.

- ➢ Figure 5.23 illustrates an example of a two-tiered storage environment. This environment optimizes the primary storage for performance and the secondary storage for capacity and cost.

- ➢ The policy engine, which can be software or hardware where policies are configured, facilitates moving inactive or infrequently accessed data from the primary to the secondary storage.

- ➢ Some prevalent reasons to tier data across arrays is archival or to meet compliance requirements.

- ➢ As an example, the policy engine might be configured to relocate all the files in the primary storage that have not been accessed in one month and archive those files to the secondary storage.

- ➢ For each archived file, the policy engine creates a small space-saving stub file in the primary storage that points to the data on the secondary storage.

➢ When a user tries to access the file at its original location on the primary storage, the user is transparently provided with the actual file from the secondary storage.

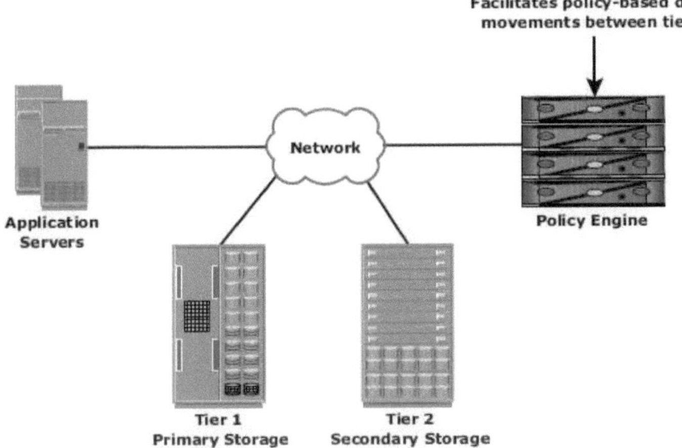

Fig 5.23: Implementation of intra-array storage tiering

Reference Books:

1 Alan Dix, Janet Finalay, Gregory D AbiwdmRusselBealel: Human-Computer Interaction, III Edition, Pearson , Education, 2008.

2 Eberts: User Interface Design, Prentice Hall, 1994

3 Wilber O Galitz: The Essential Guide to User Interface Design- An Introduction to GUI Design, Principles and Techniques, Wiley-Dreamtech India Pvt Ltd, 2011.

4. Ben Shneiderman, Plaisant, Cohen, Jacobs: Designing the User Interface, 5th Edition, Pearson ,Education, 2010.

Printed by Books on Demand GmbH, Norderstedt / Germany